100 Ways
to
Create Wealth

Also by Steve Chandler & Sam Beckford:

9 Lies That Are Holding Your Business Back

The Small Business Millionaire

Business Coaching

Also by Steve Chandler:

100 Ways to Motivate Yourself

Ten Commitments to Your Success

Reinventing Yourself

Relationshift (with Michael Bassoff)

The Joy of Selling

The Story of You

100 Ways to Motivate Others (with Scott Richardson)

The Hands-Off Manager (with Duane Black)

50 Ways to Create Great Relationships

Two Guys Read Moby-Dick (with Terrence Hill)

Two Guys Read the Obituaries (with Terrence Hill)

100 Ways
to
Create Wealth

Steve Chandler
Sam Beckford

Robert D. Reed Publishers • Bandon, OR

Robert D. Reed Publishers
P.O. Box 1992
Bandon, OR 97411
Phone: 541-347-9882 • Fax: -9883
E-mail: 4bobreed@msn.com
web site: www.rdrpublishers.com

Editor: **Cleone Lyvonne**
Cover Designer: **Cleone Lyvonne**
Typesetter: **Barbara Kruger**

ISBN 978-1-931741-78-1

Library of Congress Control Number 2006904315

Manufactured, typeset and printed in the United States of America

Dedications

From Steve to Kathy

From Sam to Val, Isabella & Benjamin,
who make me the wealthiest man alive

Acknowledgments

From Steve

To my young genius friend Sam Beckford, the true small business millionaire, for helping so many people find their way to prosperity.

To the super team of Carl, Carol and Sheryl at Gilbert Mail who exemplify and model impeccable customer service and positive attitude. To Maurice Bassett for reinventingyourself.com. To Steve Hardison for being the most powerful wealth coach on the planet, to Fred Knipe and Lynette for friendship and music and the brand new year, to Lindsay Brady for masterful hypnotherapy, to Katie and Stephen Mitchell for the best books and the best school ever imagined, to Darlene Brady for tireless numerical feats, to Michael Bassoff for RelationShift, and to Alison for our night with Patsy Cline. To Bob Reed and Cleone for making books a reality. To Ron and Mary Hulnick and the University of Santa Monica for lighting up the planet. To Reece Bawden and Dennis Deaton for founding the learning systems that started it all. To Greg Freundschuh for the Peyton Manning story.

To Kathy for everything, and to Jess, Stephanie, Mar and Bobby for having provided for me all the happiness I'll ever need.

From Sam

To my parents for teaching me about creation and the creator. To John & Greta for their support, belief, and love.

To Dave for your constantly creating. To Jose for teaching me about the "same price of nothing" and the "pigeons." To Arnold for the friendship and trust. To Steve for teaching me to own everything. To Scott Fowler a lifetime of friendship. To Scott Tigchelaar for the friendship and advice. To Ed Tigchelaar for telling me to move the decimal point. To Terence for the inspiration. To Andrew for being MacGyver helping me do the impossible. To Jason for the class act. To Laura for the extra mile. To Launa for keeping it all together.

To Dan Kennedy for giving me the three magic words. To Les Hewitt for the focus and friendship. To anyone else who I forgot to put on this list—for getting over it.

To Val, Isabella & Benjamin for the patience, the love, and the most important motivation of all.

"If you ask me to name the proudest distinction of Americans, I would choose the fact that they were the people who created the phrase *'to make money.'* No other language or nation had ever used these words before... Americans were the first to understand that wealth has to be created."

Ayn Rand

Introduction

You Can Set Yourself Free

Sam Beckford had five straight business failures before he turned it all around. These 100 "ways" represent the exact changes he made to execute the turnaround and become a millionaire. They not only worked for him, but they have also worked for hundreds of his clients who have transformed failure into success.

When we seek to help you create more wealth in life, we're not trying to make you more self-important or encourage you to find ego-gratification by the accumulation of material objects.

Our intention is to give you a rare and strange freedom—the freedom to move easily in life, go where you want to, and do what you want to do. Wealth can deliver that freedom.

We want you to find the freedom to help yourself thrive in your true purpose, to find the leverage to help loved ones, and to financially help organizations and causes you want to help.

Many people shake their heads when they hear about conditions in Africa and can't do anything except curse about it. Then they curse people who have the power to help, the people who have the freedom to send money and dig a well in Africa, but don't.

We want this book to give you a chance to *be* one of the people who have the power to help.

We are not going to be talking about clever money tricks. How to trick people into anything, or how to do quasi-pyramid schemes, or catch the latest wave of "hot opportunities." You yourself are the real opportunity available to you. You can inspire yourself to generate earned wealth, the kind of money that comes from serving the greatest number of people in the most preferred ways.

We both spend our days coaching people on their path toward greater wealth. Our clients often enjoy surprising success, and whenever they do it's always because of a breakthrough in their thinking. These breakthroughs have been listed in this book and capped at 100. We've chosen the breakthroughs that work the best and the most often. And, since this is a book about what works for others, it is also a book about what will work for you.

This is not a book about investing or money management. It is merely a recounting of our collective experience as personal coaches and business coaches. It's also the biographies of two men who went from deep debt and failure to consistent major paydays.

Creating wealth is a different concept than "discovering" a way to cash in on some wealth, or a way to take advantage of some faddish external circumstance.

We're talking about creating your wealth from within yourself. Finding that place inside where you love to be and finding that work on the outside that you love to do.

So, this book is about love and money. Don't be ashamed to follow the directions. Don't be afraid to be inspired by the ideas. The more inspired you are, the faster you will create. Traditional scriptures say we were born in the image of our creator. To what degree do we really believe that? Maybe simply to the degree that we create. Our range of wealth-creation is dependent on our belief in our capacity to create. This book was written to empower that belief.

1. Draw a Line in the Sand

When you see a successful business,
someone once made a courageous decision.

Peter Drucker

Sam Beckford likes to tell his new clients about the most defining moment of his business success and career. It happened long before he became known as "The small business millionaire."

This defining moment didn't happen at his business. It actually happened at a grocery store. Sam and his wife had finished shopping and went to pay for their groceries with his debit card, and the card didn't clear through. So he tried it again and the card didn't work again, and the cashier offered to try a third time saying, "There must be a problem with the card."

Sam said, "Yeah, I know the problem—there's no money in the account."

He was there with his wife, and they had to leave the store, and leave all their groceries to be put back on the shelves. And there was something very painful about reaching a point where he couldn't even feed his family.

"It was the most embarrassing, humiliating thing," Sam said. "And I said, 'This is never going to happen again. I'm sick of being broke. I'm sick of being poor.' I'd been trying to play the odds that there'd still be a little money left in the account. But walking out of that store that day was the turning point for all the business achievement that happened after that. It's the moment I woke up."

Sam now tells that story to a lot of people who are trying to make it as small business owners, and professionals of all kinds. Sometimes they come up to him afterwards at a seminar and say, "You know, I can identify with that grocery store story because it happened to me two weeks ago."

As for lack of wealth, we can relate. We've been there. We've been down and in debt with utterly failed careers and ventures. Probably in worse ways than you.

So don't try to push that pain away. Let yourself really feel what you are missing. Because that's when you will be focused enough to say *no* to that feeling. You can say "no" to feeling that way ever again. Now you can find a place to take a stand.

Be completely negative about what you no longer want. Refuse to let it in. Stand up to it. Draw your line in the sand, step back, and *dare it* (the old you) to ever cross that line again.

Use a moment like that to be your final resolve to say, "Never again. Never." There's a positive turning point hidden in everything. Even in something that feels that bad.

People, like Steve Chandler, who have recovered from addictions, eventually reach what they call a "bottom." They can't go any lower without dying. But once they've hit their bottom they often find new strength to say, "That's it. There's just no way that I'm going to live like this any more. I don't care what I have to do, I don't care how uncomfortable it is, I don't care what they tell me to do, I'll even go through those 12 steps. I'm doing it, because this is the end of this life."

Wealth has steps, too. Just like addiction recovery. And the steps work. And the first step is to draw a line in the sand.

2. Ask Each Day, "Why Not Me?"

For good or for ill, self-concept is destiny.

Nathaniel Branden

In life we do what we believe we can do. No more than that.

Then, based on the limits of that belief, we become stuck in our financial situation. Soon we are envying others. We create an artificial separation between ourselves and the people we envy. People we believe can do what we cannot do.

However, this separation is so flimsy it can be broken through quite easily. Because this separation is simply a thought. It's nothing real.

In our minds, and just in our minds, out of psychic self-protection, out of having an alibi for why we are not really successful, we just say, "Wealth is so far away!" Or we say, "It's unimaginable to be driving in a car like that." Or to be taking trips like that or to be putting the kids in a college like that. "It is so unimaginable that I won't even allow myself to get disappointed by thinking about it. I won't even picture myself doing it."

And because we believe we can't do it we never will.

Steve says, "There was a time when I was a boy that I didn't believe I could swim. So I didn't. And people would try to convince me to just jump in the water and it'll hold you up. And I didn't believe it. And so I didn't swim and the times I tried, it seemed like I was sinking! I got out fast! It was only after I believed it that I could do it. Thoughts are all we've got."

And yet we don't examine them.

There are people who treat wealth and success like some kind of really lucky external event that happened to them. In other words, they distance themselves from causal aspects of belief. But it's a false distance.

We have a client who, when he talks about a good month that he had, says, "Oh, I was really blessed that month."

And after a while, Steve said to him, "Do you know that you only use the term 'blessed' in reference to money? Do you realize that? Don't you believe that your life itself is a blessing? That your family is a blessing? Your ability to breathe and think are blessings, as well? How about your *ability* to have earned that wealth and to have caused it?"

But he was stuck in the mindset that said he was humbled by this astonishing blessing of money.

"I've been blessed again!"

Steve asked him, "What blessing are you now referring to?"

"Well, the good month I had in April; we made more money than in any other month. We were really blessed that month."

And he, by thinking that, kept money-making as something distant from himself. Only some divine intervention could give him money. He couldn't believe his own role in creating it for himself.

And that's a tragic elevation of money. It's putting money on a pedestal higher than your own religion or spirituality, to keep using the term "blessed" only in reference to money. And to be humbled and in awe of life only when it comes to money.

Why not have money be just like anything else? Instead of giving it religious standing. If you want to have some eggs, you'll just go *make* some eggs; and if you want to have some money, why not just go make some?

It's not something you have to be awestricken over. You don't have to put in an immediate call to the almighty when it flows in. Do you do that when water flows in? Or a breeze?

It's just cause-and-effect money we are talking about here. Serve and you shall receive. It's not something that ought to inspire tears streaming from your eyes in humble adoration. It is no different than anything else you want to make.

The blessing happens when you are born. The blessings continue when you wake up in the morning. That's when you're blessed. It's not, "I'm not blessed yet. I made my sales calls but I'm not blessed yet."

We were attending spiritual teacher Byron Katie's school and she was getting ready to teach the day's lesson, adjusting her microphone, and she sneezed. When someone in the audience said, "God bless you," she said, "You're too late."

3. Don't Wait for Perfection

Start where you are. Distant fields always look greener,
but opportunity lies right where you are.

Robert Collier

Sometimes the circumstances look all wrong. Things aren't perfect. Should we go ahead anyway? How do we decide?

Steve loves to use the example of Troy Shondell although Sam has to ask his father about the early 1960s when Shondell was a teen idol singer.

Influenced by the late Buddy Holly, Elvis, Little Richard and many more of the early rockers, Troy Shondell began his singing career while still in high school in Fort Wayne, Indiana. One of his first local recordings was "Kissin' at the Drive-In" on Mercury Records. That record became a big regional hit that gained him hope for future national attention. (Please don't say you don't remember "Kissin' at the Drive-In"!)

Troy's fame soon spread to the Chicago area where he and his band became the first rock band to ever appear at the then famous Brass Rail blues and jazz club in downtown Chicago. Troy and his band had fans standing in line to watch rock 'n' roll for the first time in downtown Chicago. However, the momentum didn't hold, and Troy bounced from small label to small label without much luck.

Then, in October of 1960, Troy's father died of a heart attack. With his father's death, Troy's mother inherited a small business that was her only income. In order to keep it going, she asked Troy to come home and help her. His dream of hit music would have to wait. So Troy quit the band and gave up music in order to help with the immediate crisis.

In February 1961 his mother encouraged Troy to audition for an extra part in a movie being filmed locally after seeing an ad in the local paper. At the audition a man familiar with Troy's music said he would finance a recording session if Troy would consider trying it again. Troy was overjoyed, especially since he had been hanging on to a special song just in case an opportunity like this came along. It was a song that a local disc jockey in Fort Wayne had called to Troy's attention. The song was called "This Time (We're Really Breaking Up)."

There was a tremendous blizzard the day of the session on April 1, 1961, in Batavia, Illinois, and only three musicians were able to make it to the session: a guitar player, a sax player, and a drummer. Should they even do this session? Where would the bass sound come from?

It didn't seem like the best time to try for a big comeback recording.

But maybe timing wasn't everything. Maybe desire and passion meant more than timing.

The session was a go. Troy played piano, vibes and worked hard to get a bass-type sound out of his guitar. He completely threw himself into a heartbreakingly great vocal performance of "This Time." They were exhausted at the end of the session, but they'd made the record. And now it was time to play it for the world.

Every record company in Chicago turned it down.

So Troy decided to start his own label. At least that way he would have an actual vinyl disk to play. And one day while visiting WJJD in Chicago, Troy tried to get airplay for the record he knew represented his future, even if it meant he had to beg. Luckily that night the DJ was a former supporter of Troy's and he took pity on the desperate singer. He got permission from the station to play "This Time" but only once and it had to be on his "Rate the Record" show, airing late in the evening. It was a gamble for Troy, because the records that lost the phone-in contest were never to be played again. Troy's record—the one recorded in the blizzard with only three musicians—won the contest! Troy's sparse and haunting "This Time" had stunned listeners with its beauty, pain, and passion. Now in rotation at that station, the record began to sell. In fact, 10,000 copies were sold the very first week! "This Time" topped the charts for an unprecedented 16 weeks during the summer of '61.

Although other successes would follow for Troy, none of the others might ever have happened without "This Time." "This Time" went on to sell over 3,000,000 copies that first year!

Many people would have used that blizzard in Illinois in April of 1961 as a reason to postpone the session. The timing wasn't right. They didn't even have a bass player! How are you going to get your bass sound? With a guitar? Bad timing if there ever was bad timing.

But Troy Shondell put enough passion into that stormy night to electrify a whole nation of teenage record buyers. Even today, the record sounds great, and the sparse and funky production values only heighten its impact. It feels raw and real. You can download the record today and crank it up. And don't miss the message as you listen.

Circumstance is nothing... passion is everything.

Every once in a while we put a little slogan up in our office that says "Doing it now is more important than doing it right." We don't mean don't do it as well as you can. We just mean if you wait until the timing is perfect, it'll never happen. Just do it now. This time.

4. Use One Hour a Day

Success and happiness are not matters of chance but choice.

Zig Ziglar

It's amazing what you have time for. Especially once you decide to *make* time for it.

People who say they "don't have time" to build up a certain skill, or get that online course of study going, or learn another language, or start a home business, are only fooling themselves.

If you had a kidney condition where you needed to get on a dialysis machine for an hour a day or get a daily blood transfusion, or do your chemotherapy, you wouldn't say, "Well, I'll just have to die, because I don't have an extra hour." You'd just say, "Fine. Only an hour? I can do that."

And you would be right. Anyone can free up an hour a day for anything. And you can put anything into that hour. Anybody has time to put something into an hour's time slot and devote the fully focused hour to it. Without losing a beat. Without losing any efficiency at all. Or any relationships.

In fact, here's the irony: if you singled out an hour for something special, the other hours of your life would probably improve! They would become *more* efficient, not less.

If you took an hour away from your life today, you would become more efficient in the other 23 hours than you were before. Because you would pay more attention to priorities. You would become more awake to your precious time.

Work expands to fill the time allotted for it.

So give yourself an hour. Start today.

What will you do for your special one hour? Can you put something in there that will create wealth for you?

Years ago, Thomas Watson, who led the original success of the early amazing IBM, had a favorite motto. It only had one word in it. The word was "Think." That was his slogan. He had it posted all around the company. He knew that the more his people remembered to do that, the faster IBM would succeed. And he was right. And the same is true in your life.

Try this: Just sit alone for an hour with a yellow pad and have it be your creative thinking time. Let whatever arises from your subconscious mind find its way to paper. Don't judge anything; just take dictation. You'll be amazed.

Most people don't *think* about what their financial possibilities are. They don't even think of where they want to go. They're so lost inside their problematic daily existence they don't make time to see the big picture. They're just doing things, always busy and running. Racing ahead. Trying in vain to get into their own future.

And when they're not doing that, they're trying to *kill time* with the TV or internet!

People who aren't really living their true lives and who aren't into what they really want to be into (which is a recommended prerequisite for real wealth creation) are trying to distract themselves from that very fact. They want to forget about how unfulfilled they are. So they use all kinds of things, including entertainment, to distract themselves from that horrible feeling.

If I'm not too happy with what I'm up to in life, I can tune in to this TV talk show and hear people yelling at each other, and hear all the bad news, and hear about the people who have gone missing, or who are trapped underground. And soon I'll follow all that with my heart in my throat! That is a way for me to tune into other people's problems as a way of not looking at my own. I'm tuning into other people's lives as a way of not living my own. Pretty soon I've got these surrogates living my life for me, on the soap opera of the evening news, in the missing person reports, in the crime shows, on sports teams, and even on the radio in my car. I'm letting these tragic people live my life for me.

Do I really need to know all that news? Do I really need to know about Russell Crowe hitting some bellman in a hotel with a phone? I only need to know about that if I'm the person suing Russell Crowe (which is the 101st way to create wealth: make Russell Crowe angry, let him hurt you, then sue him.)

Come to think of it, thinking about all that self-distracting I do, maybe I do have an hour I can devote to learning what my mind can do. Everybody has an hour. And that's all we're talking about.

5. Make Money a Game

Life is too important to be taken too seriously.

Oscar Wilde

People bring more energy to a game than they do to anything else.

Everybody at your family gathering can be tired and not want to do anything, but if somebody says, "We're going to play volleyball in the back yard!" everyone jumps up and runs out. And all of a sudden, everyone who was tired and weary and had a rough week and didn't want to do anything is yelling and having fun and running around the yard.

What just happened?

The paradigm just shifted from real life to a game. What you did was introduce a game into their lives. Games inspire higher energy. They fire up the imagination and the body has new life.

And the same paradigm shift can happen in your workday. Once you fully grasp the power of games, you'll know what to do.

Notice how people can play board games like Monopoly for hours on end. They play with great spirit and inventiveness. Video and computer games even more so. A pick-up game of basketball in the park after a long hard day at work can wake a person up like nothing else!

It's the joy of just playing. Kids want to stay up and play all night. There is no fatigue when you're playing.

Contrast that to "working."

Working grinds you down. It hits you even before you do it. Just the thought of it. Just the thought of your work-day can fill you with dread and anxiety. You're weary before you begin.

Wealth happens to us fastest when we can *play* it into existence.

But it's hard, given our history, to associate play with money. Money is often just terrifying to people. Far from seeing it as a game, people see it as survival. Money is like oxygen to them. Not to be fooled around with. Serious business. You can die from lack of it!

And that very belief system is what takes all the fun out of making it. All the joy. All the creativity.

The richest man in America, Bill Gates, has always said, "We only have one product here at Microsoft: human imagination."

But how can you fire up your imagination when you are fighting to survive? Gasping for air? Drowning in debt? Those are all just thoughts. But they are thoughts that shut off the flow of life and wealth. Wealth comes from imagination. From playful thoughts and tireless energy.

Therefore one of the fastest ways to create wealth is to quit "working." Instead of working, do something you love so much it feels like play. Like the way playing basketball felt to Michael Jordan or hosting a TV show feels to Oprah or writing Harry Potter novels felt to J.K. Rowling.

Stephen King has made hundreds of millions of dollars writing. In the morning he works passionately on his novel-in-progress with heavy metal music roaring in the background. In the afternoon he returns to work on the writing he's just *playing* with. He calls that afternoon project "my toy truck." Soon his toy truck becomes the new novel. It all begins in play. And hundreds and hundreds of millions of dollars in royalties keep flowing in.

Notice he doesn't call that afternoon project "my difficult work project." And that's why Stephen King makes the money that struggling authors don't. He plays and they work.

Our small business and personal services clients often jump ahead in sales when they make the numbers of their business a game. Once they get a game going the numbers are no longer what scares them. They become part of the play.

Most people have "the money part" of their profession be the buried part, the grim, dark part that nobody looks at. We see so many businesses where everybody hides the numbers because they don't want the employees to know they're having a bad month. So they never allow people to get involved in the very game element that could revitalize their business.

Playing games works. A game might be like, "We want 100 new customers by April 1, and we're going to put the number in the back room, and we're all going to celebrate by going to Disney World if we hit it early!" People who convert money into a game get a different kind of energy from their people than if it's just a grim, real-life kind of approach to business. It's the playful kind of energy that creates wealth.

George Bernard Shaw said, "We don't stop playing because we grow old. We grow old because we stop playing."

Money flows to the young at heart. So we want to shift work to play any chance we get. It's a mind shift to do so. Even if it's just to keep us from growing old. Also, to give us energy. Notice that when we change something from work to play, energy and creativity increase!

Steve recalls, "I noticed this working in the factory in Detroit when I was young—making pieces on the assembly line. How dull and fatiguing—until my coworker and I decided to play a game. We would have a contest to see who could make the most pieces (we inserted wires into metal boxes) in the next hour. Loser buys dinner. GO! And boy was it fun then, going like crazy, looking over at each other to see how many pieces we had stacked up. It was really fun. And we had so much new energy for it because we were playing a game now, whereas before we were just working. We were just growing old."

6. Learn Your Process

It is not enough to want to succeed.
You must make it your conscious purpose to succeed.

Nathaniel Branden

After Sam failed five times he decided to study every successful business case history he could get his hands on. He applied what he learned. He studied, for example, the history of McDonald's.

"A big realization for me, with McDonald's, was that a lot of their wealth as a company came from real estate ownership," Sam said. "McDonald's is the largest commercial property owner next to the Catholic Church! And that's when I made the decision to focus on trying to own the real estate that my own small dance and music studio businesses run from. It was good enough for McDonald's, and it's also worked for us!"

Even learning the profit process has a fear factor, though. Because when the media and the culture demonize the free enterprise system and make you think that wealth-creation is nothing other than what greedy capitalists know how to do, then it's easy to become intimidated by the workings of successful businesses.

As a result of this intimidation, most people who go into business for themselves *almost don't want to know* how business works! They buy into all the Hollywood and media stories about back room deals making people rich. Stories that emphasize that wealth is not open to the average person. It's all about who you know. It's all about corruption.

And the more you buy into that, the less you want to learn, because you don't believe it matters what you learn. You think it's mysterious. Fortune has to favor you. You start to believe in things like "nothing but location," or "It's nothing but grabbing the economy when it's on the upswing," and all the serendipitous trendy superstitions that cynical people grab onto. But all these approaches run counter to truly *learning to earn*.

Yes, you can learn to earn.

But if you don't make that commitment to actually figure out how your business or career is going to make money, you just won't make money.

If you're not willing to get fascinated with your business and fall in love with its inner process for wealth-creation, you will not succeed. You have to really want to take your watch apart and then put it all back together again if you want be a watchmaker.

Many people say that they just don't have a mind for business. They're not being honest. There are brain surgeons doing surgery today who weren't born with a mind for brain surgery. Anything can be learned.

"I used to chase moneymaking schemes," Sam confesses today. "Schemes that said you could immediately get rich by doing some exciting thing and making all this money! But I never really understood how those opportunities worked. Remember all the multi-level marketing plans of the 90s and 80s? Basically, people would stand up at a flip chart and start drawing circles all over the place and lines that connect the circles, and then four more circles under there, and the truth is, I never actually understood how that worked either."

And that was the fatal flaw. Without understanding how a moneymaking process works, there will be no sustainable way to make it work.

"I believe that you have to understand how the money is made before you make it," Sam said. "Because if it's like a black box of mystery, if you don't have a proven system and income stream, you have a fluke."

So it's important to understand *how* your money will be made. And if you start a wealth-creation project and you can't sit down and explain the profitability process to someone in fifth grade, you should be concerned. You might not have something that you can keep going.

That's why a lot of attempts at moneymaking schemes have failed. People got involved with processes they didn't understand. Like the dot.com craze and the internet stock boom. No one ever understood how the money was to be made. People were spellbound by the internet but they never really learned *how* those ventures would earn. They invested wildly with no basic understanding that customers would have to be served and made loyal. They learned to attract people to a website, but they didn't have that basic understanding of how a profitable business would follow that up, so it all collapsed.

Other people during that ill-fated craze became experts at attracting venture capitalists to their excitement, and that became their whole product! Their ability to sell venture capitalists on their excitement! But after that stage, they were stumped.

So if you're in the restaurant business or if you're a coach or if you're a massage therapist, you really want to *learn* how people who succeed at that business do it. Exactly *what do they do* when they expand their business? Add another therapist? Increase their coaching fees? Increase the hours the restaurant is open? Or whatever they do to start to be more successful. How do they do it and how does it work?

Knowledge is earning power. Make sure you understand the process of your business: how you make money and how you can build on the process to progressively create more wealth.

7. Give It Away Before You Get It

We make a living by what we get,
but we make a life by what we give.

Winston Churchill

To a lot of people wealth is how much you *have*. But if you truly want to create wealth, you might want to change that viewpoint.

Try thinking of true wealth as how much you *give*.

Wealth is not what you can cling to. Wealth is a flowing. It flows in and out, in and out. Think of the waves on the ocean. The power of a tsunami.

That's why we recommend that you don't wait to give it away. The give and take happen together, not one after the other. And one of the reasons giving it away before you get it works is that it takes you away from thinking of money in terms of scarcity. And it takes you away from trying to cling to money, as in "I've got to grab it and bury it in the back yard!"

Even the greatest cynic can be made to understand that when you don't have psychological hang-ups about losing your money, you're going to make more money and make it faster. That's undeniable. Because without hang-ups it's easier to charge more, ask for more, and take more imaginative leaps. And so even at that basic level, this works.

Giving before you get makes it okay, on a subconscious level, for you to have large sums of money coming in. You'll be less likely to secretly sabotage your wealth inflow.

Do people really do that? Sabotage? Yes. Most people have a secret aversion to making a lot. Do you? If you do, you're not alone, but why fight that all your life?

If you make a decision to give it away before you get it, it's a lot easier to lose that subconscious undertow that sabotages your success. Now your feeling about money is elevated. No more irrational guilt or fear. Money is yours to give. This makes it a lot easier to bring money into your life.

Giving also allows you to strengthen your prices with a clear conscience. You know the incoming wealth is always going to a good cause. Therefore, you're not inappropriately focused on whether your own poor customer can afford it.

So call a great charitable cause and make a pledge—one that means something to you personally. That's giving before you get. And sit down with your partner or just with yourself and figure out who's going to get that certain per cent of glad giving you're going to do. Contact them, get their contact info, and as money comes to you, make sure it goes out to them. You can do this exciting planning before a penny comes in. That planning is part of the giving process: it's how you'll give before you get. You do it in your mind. Then your mind gets freed up.

There's a group Sam donates money to that builds wells in Africa. If you give them $8,000, there's a government-matching program that triples the money.

He had heard a presentation on how a lot of the diseases that are preventable in the world today are linked to the water supply. If kids don't have clean water, they're susceptible to a lot of diseases and death. But if you change the water supply in a village and make it clean, pure and available, then you eliminate many future problems. So if you give $8,000 to this organization, the government will triple the amount to $24,000, which is the amount it actually takes to construct a well.

"When I make a good sale of something and get an extra $8,000 in profit, I never feel guilty about that," says Sam. "Instead I'm thinking, 'Wow, I can do triple the good with this money by sending it to Africa.' So if anyone ever tells me that rich people are selfish, it just rolls off my back."

This kind of giving gives you the internal permission to make a lot of money because you know inside you can be trusted with it to do good. Money finds an easier flow to a place where it's going to be treated well. And treating money well is not keeping it and hoarding it. It's giving a portion of it away.

Even before you get it, give yourself time to plan your giving. Write that plan down. Where am I going to start donating money when it comes in? Could you give five percent of everything that came in? We've never known of anyone who couldn't live on 95 percent of what was coming in. Soon you'll always be looking into funding good causes for your five percent giving program (and many people, once they feel the beauty and bounty of this policy, up their giving to ten percent and later even more) because you've shifted your thinking from scarcity to abundant giving.

Why don't more people do this?

It's the emotion. People fear that they would be setting themselves up for disappointment. They don't want to indulge in grandiosity. They don't want to be a big shot about giving money away before they even know if they're going to *make it* in this business!

But that's exactly what this concept is going to open up for you. By pre-planning your giving, you will eliminate that fearful thinking and make yourself more creative and open to creating wealth. You'll get that flow going and remove the negative, fearful charge from money. You'll take the psychic guilt out of making money because you can feel its circular energy coming in to you and flowing out to your good causes. Rather than being clung to, money is now going to you, through you, and out to other people in need. Your self-concept expands. It embodies flow.

You can think of giving wealth away as spirituality or karma, or even notice that it lines you up with the laws of the universe. If you believe in a divine master plan, this is your way into it. Once you're in that right place mentally and spiritually, the money will come to you, and this process is the way to get it started.

8. Win Your Own Lottery

Twenty years from now you will be more disappointed by the things that you didn't do than by the ones you did do. So throw off the bowlines. Sail away from the safe harbor. Catch the trade winds in your sails. Explore.

Mark Twain

We wrote our novel *The Small Business Millionaire* about a restaurant owner and chef named Frank who didn't understand the value he was creating. (Frank was a composite of the clients we coach who are asleep to the value they create.)

Frank can go to a grocery store, buy $10 worth of ingredients, and take them back to his little restaurant to make them into a $30 meal. He's just created $20 of value. Just by the skill he puts into it.

If you cut down a tree and you take that thing that was just a tree and cut it into different boards, and you take those boards and make them into a fine piece of furniture that sells for $1,000, you've created $1,000 worth of value. (Make sure you re-plant the tree.)

Whereas, before, that value just didn't exist.

Value is created by the things we do. People were created to create. Many people say, "Oh, I couldn't run a business or do something like that, I'm bad when it comes to money." Yet that same person will go into a garden and plant things, grow things, and make something out of nothing.

Or he will create an agreement between previously disputing family members. Or create warmth and assurance for a frightened child. At our best, we are always creating.

People who think they can't create great wealth in their lives will then show you a room they've repainted, or they'll go out back and show you a birdhouse they've made.

If you were created in the image of your creator, then you were meant to create. It's as simple as that. All the instincts are already in you. You have it in you to become a small business millionaire or whatever you want to become financially. It's in you. It isn't outside of you somewhere, in the latest hot business. It's inside.

Sam is never off duty as a great teacher of success. That's not always good news to people who are just trying to make it through the day. If you see Sam coming, either duck down the alley and go the other way, or be ready to talk about how success happens.

Recently Sam walked into a convenience store at a gas station, and the woman who was behind the counter asked him if he wanted to buy a lottery ticket.

"No, that's okay, thanks. I don't need to win the lottery," Sam said. "Do you realize that every person that works at even the minimum wage is going to make more than $1 million in the course of their lifetime? So the truth is, we've already won the lottery just by living in this country."

The clerk rolled her eyes and walked away.

A lot of people are just waiting for the lottery to happen to them. There are lottery billboards that advertise "Next drawing: $4 million. Could you imagine??" And now whenever Sam sees the sign he thinks, "Yes I can imagine! But I don't play lotteries anymore because, believe it or not,

I think that winning the lottery would be a de-motivator. It would actually be disappointing because I would think, 'Oh, shoot, now I can't do this for myself!'"

When you say you'd love to "win the lottery," consider that if you're walking around on this green earth, you've already won the lottery. The odds of you even being here are trillions to one. Of everything coming together to create you. So you've already won the lottery. Don't try to win some artificial money lottery when you won't know what to do with the money.

And also be mindful of the odds. Many people say that the lottery is God's way of punishing people who are bad at math. The odds of winning are so against you. You're more likely to have an asteroid land on your house.

The truth is, you probably wouldn't even enjoy the money if you did win. Surveys show that over 70 percent of lottery winners wish they hadn't won because of what occurs with all this unearned money in their life. It becomes a nightmare.

Gandhi said unearned money was one of the real evils of the world. It makes the recipient crazy. And it takes incentive away and it robs you of the adventure and the fun and the joy and the self-esteem and everything connected to being a causal factor in creating wealth.

It's one of the subtle things that's different in our approach than popular presentations like "The Secret." Although "The Secret" is a wonderful dramatization of the role of the mind in creating success, it also suggests you will *become* rich *or have it happen to you* after enough inner visualization. Use your easy chair as a space ship and mentally sail into your own future. Picture your dreamed-up paradise enough times and wealth will be magically attracted to you. But when we say there are ways to create wealth, we really mean you can actively *create* it. By taking actions.

"The Secret" was a major step forward in dramatizing how toxic it is to always worry, and always picture what you *don't* want. It was also the best dramatization of the true power of the human mind we've ever seen. We've given copies of it to clients who are stuck in fear. Not realizing that worry is making things worse. (Worry is a misuse of the imagination.)

But remember, too, that you can be the causal factor. That doesn't mean you just "attract" wealth, because there are countless dreamy books on how to attract money through visualization and fervent hoping, and we haven't met any people for whom that alone is enough.

Creating wealth asks that we create dramatic service and value. You don't want to rob yourself of the joy of creating in this lifetime. You don't have to start a business to do it either. You can be an employee in a huge organization and start right there. Everyone you talk to is a potential customer of yours.

9. Get Out of Your Own Future

If you want to be miserable, get yourself a future.

Byron Katie

It's fine to have big plans and dreams, but wealth is created now. Right now. In this present moment. It was never created at any other time in history. It was always now.

So once your plans are reviewed, get out of your future and into this moment. This conversation you are about to have is the important one. There are hidden opportunities in every moment, and we miss them if we're always thinking ahead.

Allow all your dreams of doing great work, being creative, and making a difference in people's lives to happen today. Not in some far-off conditional future. Start where you are.

Noted psychiatrist Stanislav Grof says in *The Consciousness Revolution*, "I have worked with people who had a major goal in life that required decades of intense and sustained effort to achieve. And when they finally succeeded, they became severely depressed because they expected something that the achievement of the goal could not give them. Joseph Campbell called this situation, 'getting to the top of the ladder and finding that it stands against the wrong wall.'"

Don't put off your fulfillment. Don't put your happiness at the top of some ladder you have to climb. Don't wait until you've "made it" to feel great about life. Wealth is attracted to people who feel great *right now*. People who know how to use this moment.

When people tell you that they hope you reach your potential, they are usually talking about the future.

But the best use of your potential is not in the future. It's now. Because your potential is just another word for your talent. And the best use of your talent is right here right now. (What is your talent? Well…what do you love to do?)

This whole "potential" racket has a lot of people annoyed and depressed to be on their death beds without ever having reached it, like it was a distant star, or a brass ring on the carousel.

Your potential is not out there in your future. It's in you now. When people see your potential, they are seeing something that's already in you. Otherwise they couldn't see it. People can't see into the future. But they can see something in you. So, your true potential is not on some faraway star in a distant galaxy out there in the future. It's right here. Right now. You can use it today.

When we coach clients who are frustrated by their lack of money, our first task is to slow them down. We find that they are passing over golden opportunities right in front of them. When they tell us they need new clients, we slow them down to look at the list of existing clients. There are so many more ways those already-existing people could be served. Our clients are pressed for cash flow because they allow their brains to spend 90 percent of the time fretting about the future.

One client was a professional speaker and sales trainer we will call Jill. Jill wanted coaching on how to increase her income dramatically, so we began by looking at her calendar. We knew by listening to Jill talk that her brain was wrung out at the end of each day because she worried. When a person uses her brain for worrying, it's a misuse. It's an abuse of the brain. It would be like using your computer as a doorstop.

Jill showed Steve her calendar and Steve said, "Let's slow your rapid life down for a moment. Tell me what this is here. You've written the words, "Bank Keynote."

"Oh, that's a keynote speech I'm giving. It's okay. $6,000. I need more of those. Three of those a month and I'd be where I want to be. I guess I need to send my DVD and brochure to more banks."

"Slow down."

"Slow down?"

"Why do they want a keynote?"

"I don't know. The bank is having a sales retreat. I guess sales are down in this territory. They always have keynote speeches at these things."

We suggested that Jill had more business than she realized, but because her mind was always racing ahead wherever she was, it was probably racing ahead when she talked to the top person at the bank about this keynote. We asked her to go back in and find out why they wanted the keynote, what they hoped it would accomplish, why they were having their event, what they hoped the retreat would accomplish, and 20 more questions.

A week later Jill came back rather stunned. The bank manager told her all kinds of objectives they had for the event and revealed a long list of problems their team was facing. Some of those problems, like telephone sales skills, community relations and referral acquisition were subjects that Jill was experienced in teaching. She came out of that meeting with enough information about the bank's immediate needs to write a proposal for a year's training program. Two months later they approved it, and Jill had a contract for more than 15 times the amount she got for the keynote.

All because she slowed down, stayed in the moment, and took her time. After a year of coaching, Jill finally saw that everything she ever wanted was always right in front of her. She's been going too fast through life to see it, always trying to get into her own future, like a cat chasing its own shadow.

The present moment is paved with gold. Just like the streets of heaven. It's only the future that's bleak and frightening. Stay out of it.

10. Don't be a Wealth Wannabe

Wealth, like happiness, is never attained
when sought after directly.
It comes as a by-product of providing a useful service.

Henry Ford

One of the fastest ways to go broke is to try to get rich quick.

One of the biggest enemies of true wealth creation is getting sucked into the latest moneymaking scheme. Or real estate trend. Or hot new thing. Don't let yourself get hooked into the idea that you're going to stumble into the one magic key that's going to lead to easy money. And [a] lot of those schemes floating around. Surf [t]he infomercials on TV and you'll find them.

[... of] these wealth-wannabe schemes are self-[... be]cause they give you the false hope that you can [... s]ource outside yourself and create prosperity [... ov]ernight.

[... I'm n]ot saying you can't make money easily and [... yo]u can—but be very wary of an appeal that says, just get in now and we'll do all the work for you!"

Be wary of thinking you might get lucky this way. Luck is not something you want to associate with wealth. Luck and true, enduring wealth have no relationship to each other whatsoever.

You will see infomercials every day on TV selling you the hot new "opportunity." But what they are really selling you is your own gullibility. They're handing it back to you on a silver platter.

So when you see TV ads offering you franchises or machines that will make you money, you can be sure that what they are selling you is your own yearning for a quick fix.

And we all know the illegal pyramid schemes that have been going on forever. One person talks to you about how they've made $50,000 already, and if you get in soon enough and sign enough other people up quickly, you'll make a fortune---just don't break the chain! But the math will catch up to you, if the law doesn't, because no one is being served. Service is the way to wealth, not shrewd schemes.

Look at the enormous popularity of gambling! Gambling is playing on people's wealth-wannabe sickness, the get-rich-quick dream that says maybe I can be rich without doing any work. The casinos know that the math will catch up with you there, too. No one is being served.

All these wealth-wannabe schemes also have the fatal flaw of taking *you* out of the equation. If you want to create real wealth in your life, you must honor yourself as part of the equation. You must build your personal wealth-producing strengths. Consciously and proactively. No luck is involved because no luck is necessary. No "hot new thing" need apply.

Putting the focus on the hot thing instead of yourself stops you from asking yourself, "What am I good at? What do I love doing? What do I have to offer the world? How can my talents help people? How can I serve?"

Like the great sales teacher Zig Ziglar always says, you can have anything you want in life if you help enough other people get what *they* want.

When you read true success stories, like Dave Thomas of Wendy's, or Ray Kroc at McDonalds, or the Home Depot owners, or even Bill Gates and Microsoft, there was never really a hot moneymaking scheme involved up front. For the first few years, there was a lot of failure and tough work, but it was their inner personal vision that always paid off. That and a desire to serve the most people they could in the best possible way.

Serving others by doing what you love to do is your way to wealth. Don't let anyone lure you away from it.

11. Stop Right Where You Are

Pack my bags, going to Mexico.

Steve Miller Band

Sam used to think, when he was younger and trying to go out and conquer the world and make money, that he would have to travel to a more opportune place.

"I was going to go to Mexico," he said, "because that was supposed to be one place that was hot and happening. Then sometime after that I thought I'd have to get myself to China somehow because Amway was going to open in China, and I thought, 'Wow! One billion Chinese in my multi-level pyramid!' Then at one time I was going to go to New Zealand. There was a long distance phone service opening there that looked good. So I thought, 'I have to go over there; that's where the money's going to be!' And then I even looked at going to Chile because I thought that was going to be where it was happening."

Sam now admits he was insane.

But it's not uncommon to be insane about "where the money is." We all have that lingering thought that the opportunity might be a little greener on the other side of the hill.

And there's that great book called *Acres of Diamonds* by Russell Conwell that dramatically addresses this very insanity. His little book, which you can (and should) read in less than an hour's sitting, originated as a speech, which Conwell delivered over 6,000 times around the world! Just one speech over and over, always making a huge impact on the minds of his audiences.

Conwell's central idea is that one need not look elsewhere for opportunity, achievement, or fortune—the resources to achieve all good things are present in your own community. His speech was inspired by a true story once told to Conwell by an Arab guide, about a man who wanted to find diamonds so badly that he sold his property and went off in futile search for them; then the man he sold his property to discovered that a rich diamond mine was located right there underground. Right on the property. Conwell elaborated on the theme through examples of success, genius, service, and other virtues involving ordinary Americans contemporary to his audience. "Dig in your own back yard!" he would yell out at the end.

You can find the text of this inspiring speech online. He used the wealth from that one speech to eventually found and fund Temple University in Philadelphia.

When Sam stopped looking around at all these opportunities in far-off lands, and simply opened a little music and dance studio right where he was, he found his own acres of diamonds. Today he knows many people who have left his community to pursue an opportunity elsewhere. And the new area they're in? What a surprise that it wasn't the gold mine they thought it would be.

When we consult with people in less-populated areas like Montana or Wyoming or Iowa, they'll often say, "If I were in a state like California, then my business would do really well, because in California they have so many advantages, and the population, the people there have so much money. It would be terrific!"

Then there was Teresa in California who was saying to us if she were in a state like Connecticut, where it was smaller and not as busy and not as expensive to do business, then she'd finally be successful. Because you know, being in California is harder because it's so populated by others wanting to succeed.

We're not saying don't ever move. But don't think you have to, either. There's opportunity right where you are, even more so than before, because we're in such an interconnected, global community now. With the internet, it really doesn't matter where you are. That last website you visited to buy something. Where was it? New York? Idaho? Who cares? We buy books and CDs from Amazon, right? (Maybe even this one.) And where is Amazon? Who knows?

You're at the center of the world, wherever you are.

So be somewhere you really want to be. Because you're going to do a better business that way. If you really want to be close to your family, or back in a town that you enjoy and feel like you belong in, then you'll be a part of the community.

Don't just be somewhere because you imagine that the business opportunities are better there. Start in a place where you love living and you love being. (For some, that's a busy metropolis with lots of energy, and for others it's not.) Get your lifestyle in alignment with your successful career. Have it all work for you. Don't say, "Someday when we're successful we can live where we really want to." Start wherever you want.

12. Boycott Charles Dickens

Money, which represents the prose of life, and which is hardly
spoken of in parlors without an apology, is in its effects and
laws, as beautiful as roses.

Ralph Waldo Emerson

The miserly villains in Charles Dickens novels grab for
money at the expense of poor human beings. The Dickens
novels may have set the tone for the whole Western culture's view of rich people.

Even today it carries forward. In the movies it's the evil
villain that's the rich guy, and it's always the big moneyed
corporation that's out to victimize the little guy. Dickens
started that trend.

But to attract wealth and be peaceful inside, you have to
set your copy of Dickens down and write your own book.

The great poet John Milton said, "The mind is its own
place, and in itself can make a heaven of hell, or a hell of
heaven."

First of all, money is a good thing. You can help people
if you have money. Some problems can only be solved with
money. All the wonderful foundations that save the environment, protect animals, help educate poor people, and
cure diseases are not funded by poor people.

And the whole Charles Dickens mindset, that people with money are the oppressors, has a lot of sour grapes in it. Instead of "That could be me!" people are thinking, "I wouldn't want to be like rich people are." And soon there is a negative mythology around rich people.

The irony is that the people who are the most persistent in perpetuating the stereotype are the very Hollywood actors and directors who are making $20 million a film. They grow rich starring in the movie that tries to portray rich people as being evil for accepting so much money for what they do.

It's no wonder that people get so confused about this subject. And it does not help your own prosperity to blindly accept the Charles Dickens stereotype.

Because you're not going to want to become something that is despised by even you!

With your children it's especially important to eliminate the stereotype. You want to make sure that your kids don't think that rich people are automatically bad people. Parents pass down their own bitter, jealous feelings about people with money. They often use their nastiest voices to say things like, "Oh, those people? Oh *yeah*, they're really *rich*." And the child can hear the contempt in the voice.

Was it envy or rage or bitterness or fear that made money evil? Spiritual teacher Byron Katie has freed many people from their "money issues" and helped them to fully enjoy watching the ebb and flow of wealth without worrying about any of it. As Katie has said, "Money is a wonderful metaphor. It flows from here to there, through all countries, through phone systems and wires. It shows us how to be, mentally: how to flow, how not to have any barriers, how to take all forms. It shows us how easy it is to come in and leave all the time. It's a great guru. If you did what money does, you would be completely in love with what is." (From *Work and Money* by Byron Katie: www.thework.com.)

Society offers your brain a wealth vocabulary and a poverty vocabulary. Whichever one you choose to think and speak with will have a major influence on your success.

Because you can actually end up *sentencing yourself* to wealth or poverty with the sentences you form in your mind and in your chosen conversations.

When you speak, every cell in your body listens in. Your subconscious mind files your words away as reality. And you can test that language-to-reality process out for yourself at any time. Just repeat certain words and phrases, such as "I'm getting really sleepy, I'm getting really sleepy," and feel what happens. You'll start to yawn; you'll actually start to get sleepy. You might try saying, "I can taste lemons in my mouth" and all of a sudden your mouth will pucker up and you'll feel the sour taste. These experiments will show you that whatever it is you're thinking and speaking has a tremendous impact on all the chemistry in your system, whether you think you "believe" it completely or not.

So it's a great wealth-encouraging practice to reverse yourself when you catch yourself using the language of the poor. Catch yourself before you say, "Oh, we'll never afford that." And then say, "Well, wait a minute, that's not really true. There's a good chance we *could* afford it soon. I'm really good at what I do." You can always revise what you've just said. Let your words pay tribute to your ability to create wealth through your own thinking. As Napoleon Hill taught us, we really can think and grow rich. All of us. (And that was his whole point. It doesn't take a genius to get rich. The average person can think and grow rich.)

Language isn't just some superficial communication form. It is the mental process that creates our unique world. We speak our world into existence.

To do anything you first have to think it, and then when you *say* it, that reinforces it further, and soon you're actually doing it. But in the beginning, there was the word. If you sentence yourself to an early disconnect by not being able to even *think* the things you will do, it's going to be hard (if not impossible) to actually do them.

Everyone who's experienced hypnotherapy and hypnotism knows that if you can get language into the brain that says it's not possible to raise your arm, you really can't raise your arm. A skilled hypnotherapist can bypass the left side of the brain and go directly to the right brain, saying "Your eyelids are heavy," or "Your legs are cold and they cannot move, and you will not be able to get up from this chair," and it really happens that you can't.

So whatever you tell yourself is possible will literally become what is possible.

Stop talking about the bad economy, or "How I just can't win." Don't talk about how the little guy always gets shortchanged. Don't say, "It's who you know." That's all poverty language.

Our habitual words about wealth and success also become frozen into attitudes. So as a test over the next couple of days, listen to what people say and how they speak about certain things. Ask people what they think of the internet, and notice how they respond. Or ask people what they think of the economy or the community they live in, and notice how they respond. That'll tell you a lot about whether someone's speaking the language of the poor. It will also explain a lot about their position in life.

Or as Napoleon Hill put it, "Our brains become magnetized with the dominating thoughts which we hold in our minds, and, by means with which no one is familiar, these 'magnets' attract to us the forces, the people, the circumstances of life which harmonize with the nature of our dominating thoughts."

From now on you can start challenging the truth of all poverty thoughts. You can replace them with magnetic, wealth-inspiring thoughts. Instead of, "I have to do this," you'll say, "I'm choosing to do this." Instead of "problems" you'll now work with "games, projects and fascinatingly challenging situations." You'll replace "I'm trying to get through this" with "There's a lot I can get *from* it." The language of victimization and obligation ("I should") will be replaced with the language of *intention*. ("I want to, I choose to, I will.")

Will I succeed at creating wealth in my life? I want to. I choose to. And I will.

13. Turn Boring Business Into Art

I like boring things.

Andy Warhol

Twenty years ago if you'd have told someone that two of the greatest performing businesses in recent history would be a hardware store and a coffee shop, they'd think you were on some kind of drug.

But Home Depot and Starbucks took boring businesses and made them exciting. Twenty years ago, no one thought a hardware store could be that exciting. However, Home Depot did something to make it exciting. They rejuvenated the whole idea of how fun it is to do the work yourself. Just because hardware was an industry that existed for a long time didn't mean it wasn't a huge opportunity for wealth.

When it comes to wealth creation, people always think that they have to pick something exciting. Like the conversation you hear at the cocktail parties.

"I'm into what's happening now. Genetic nano information! I got in just in time."

"Wow, you're in that?! That must be great."

But boring industries have some advantages over the hot-sounding futuristic industries. First of all, if something is a boring industry, it has probably existed for a while, so it has an established market, and people already use the product or service, so you won't have to wait for it to catch on. You don't have to project where it will be 10 years from now. A boring, established industry is something that's been around for 30 years, and there's a great chance that it will also be around 30 more years from now.

When Sam and his wife Val started their studio business, the commonplace nature of it helped create wealth for them. It was a "boring" business, teaching kids music and dance classes. Not a hot new glamorous sounding business on the surface, at all. That service and that business had existed for a thousand years! Just teaching people how to play an instrument and how to dance. But their dedication and innovation made it exciting. And turned Sam into a millionaire.

Wayne Huizenga has owned the Miami Dolphins, the Florida Marlins, Blockbuster, and many companies that have made him millions. But he started in garbage collection! And built from there.

The other secret here is that there really are no boring industries. They're only boring when you put them to the Cocktail Party Test. But once you get inside them, it's amazing how fun and fascinating you can make them.

Look at what Andy Warhol did with the soup can!

Because he was at times bed-ridden and sickly as a child, Andy Warhol became an outcast among his schoolmates. As he lay in bed he used to draw, listen to the radio, and collect pictures of movie stars that he put on the bedroom wall. Looking back later, Warhol described that period of his childhood as influential in the development of his intriguing reclusive personality and in the forming of his artistic interests.

Wealth can start anywhere when the mind stays open.

It was during the 1960s that Warhol transformed himself from an advertising illustrator into one of the most famous American artists who ever lived. Andy Warhol helped define the decade in modern pop art.

He took the boring out of boring and made it fascinating. Warhol began to make paintings of famous (but dull!) American products such as Campbell soup cans. He soon switched to silkscreen prints that he produced serially, seeking not only to make art of mass-produced items but to mass produce the art itself. Warhol said he wanted to be "a machine." He minimized the role of his own creative insight in the production of his work and thereby sparked a revolution in art—his work quickly became very controversial, and popular.

Soon there were Warhol dollar bills, celebrities, brand name products, and images from newspaper clippings. He used material that was already there in front of everyone. Nothing new. Such as plain old boring Coca-Cola bottles. Warhol said, "What's great about this country is that America started the tradition where the richest consumers buy essentially the same things as the poorest. You can be watching TV and see Coca-Cola, and you know that the President drinks Coke, Liz Taylor drinks Coke, and just think, you can drink Coke, too. A Coke is a Coke and no amount of money can get you a better Coke than the one the bum on the corner is drinking. All the Cokes are the same and all the Cokes are good. Liz Taylor knows it, the President knows it, the bum knows it, and you know it."

Warhol later founded *Interview* magazine and published *The Philosophy of Andy Warhol* (1975) in which he declared, "Making money is art, and working is art and good business is the best art."

Warhol had so many possessions it took Sotheby's nine days to auction his estate after his death for a total gross amount of over US $20 million. His total estate was worth considerably more.

He was one of the greatest pop artists who ever lived, and successful because he loved what, to other people, was boring.

So half the fun of work is what you bring to it. Whether you can transform it from a mere job to a work of art, making each day your masterpiece.

14. Switch from Need to Want

Everything you want is out there waiting for you to ask. Everything you want also wants you. And you have to take action to get it.

Jules Renard

I really need this job. I need this money. So I have to go along, I have to sell myself, I have to turn away opportunities because I have to. I can't afford to say no to this.

Familiar? It's the incessant internal dialogue of need. All the things I need to do. All the things I absolutely have to do.

We were coaching a business a year ago that had a problem employee we will call Willie who was also a top money-producer and sales person. The small business owner Aaron kept saying, "Willie is just bad for my business—taking up a whole lot of my mental energy. On the other hand, he's a profitable person to keep. He's a big producer. So we *need* Willie. We can't just let him go. It's going to cost the business all this money if we do, and we can't really afford to do that."

Aaron thought he needed Willie. And as in all professional relations, need is toxic. It is psychologically dysfunctional and it never ends well. Not in our experience.

Finally the owner Aaron made the decision just to say "No, we're not going to operate from a position of need; we're going to start operating from a position of *want*—living in the inquiry: 'What do we really *want* this company to be?'"

He made that tough decision to let Willie go—at a very inopportune time! And it did cost Aaron a fair amount of cash flow, short term. However, looking back later he was happy because the action he took broke through the whole psychological barrier of need. After that Aaron never let his "needs" govern his actions. He ran his business based on his wants. Not only that, but the new person who filled Willie's place had the production back to Willie's level in less than three months.

Your whole mind goes weak whenever you think in terms of need. And a weak mind does not create.

A lot of the small companies we work with have their whole business set up based on trying to continuously *fill their needs.* So they have meetings based on "What do we need to do? What positions do we *need* to fill?" After these fear-based meetings, anxious employees scatter anxiously throughout the building trying to fill all the unmet needs.

These meetings are poisoned with the word "need." "What kind of inventory do we *need* to stock given the urgent jobs we have coming up?"

It's all a fearful reaction to life.

It's completely reaction-based rather than creation-based and the whole purpose of our coaching and consulting is to help people create wealth instead of just filling needs. Success is a creation. It's not an unfulfilled need.

When we can get an individual or a small company to switch their conversation from needs to wants they surge ahead. We switch from *what do we need to do?* to *what's our desire?*

The more people are willing to put words and pictures to their ideal scene, the faster it becomes reality. Without it, your mind can't serve you. The mind does not solve general problems or achieve vague or general goals. An ideal scene is full of color and precision, like a Chinese painting.

Enlightened wealth creators start their meetings this way: What do we want to create? What do we want to produce? All of a sudden everything changes and they get out ahead of the curve and they start anticipating opportunities. *Now* they are profitable.

Need takes your energy away. Ayn Rand said it (it's the quote in the front of this book) best, that America was the first country to ever use the phrase "make money." Everyone else always referred to money in some other subservient, obsequious way like it comes to you, you get lucky, you're blessed by it, or some kind of humble, victimized relationship to receiving it from on high. America was the first country to ever step up and say, "We're simply going to *make* some money" which inserted that one little psychological strength that made America really get it: You can *produce* wealth. You can *create* financial well-being. It was no accident that America soon led the world in the production of goods.

Other nations were thinking that you had to re-distribute a finite amount of money. All the socialist countries of the world were trying to re-distribute the limited amount of money that was already in existence, whereas America just started creating money out of innovative products and service. Money was generated by imagination in ever-increasing multiples, allowing the human ingenuity to expand outward like the universe itself after the big bang.

Switching from need to want is a version of that same big bang. You can explode your whole culture by this switch. For example you can ask, "How do we *want* our team meetings to go?" instead of "What do we *need* to cover?" Do we want to call a meeting based on identifying our needs and our problems? Or do we want to get out ahead of the curve and ask, "What do we want to produce and create in the next week and how can we do that?"

The more you think in terms of needs, the needier you get. You lose your sense of inner peace and strength. Now it's all worry all the time. Like a 24-hour radio station between your ears, all worry all the time. You are fearful you're not going to get what you need. You inner broadcast is: "I need a new person. I need customers. I need money. I need a loan. I need a break." You are unnecessarily stressed out because you've created a frantic life of running around to get your needs met. There's no creation in that. There's no invention. There's no loving service of others. None of the things that create wealth happen when you're trying to fulfill unmet needs.

Once you shift your mind over to the category of wants, you start getting creative. You're then more *in charge*! You're doing something you *want*. When I say I *want* more clients than I have, it becomes a want rather than a need, and it very subtly shifts my whole life.

There's yet another downside in thinking and living in reaction to perceived needs. It's the shutting down that happens to your energy when a perceived need is no longer present. Need-fulfillment behaves just like an addiction. Without a need, you don't take any action! Instead you think, "I don't really *need* that, so I shouldn't write it down as something that I'm going to go acquire or accomplish; I don't really need it." And now you're not going for it because you don't "need" it.

When you ask yourself what you *want*, you can be unlimited in that thinking. You're not limited to the grim world of needs and basic survival. If you just sat down and asked yourself, at the start of the day, "What do I need?" that will produce a very limited list, and a very limited life.

Most people fall into this needs addiction because they always equate money with survival. "I need to pay the mortgage payment this month or else I won't be in the house. I need a roof over my head, or I'll die in the winter.

So that's what I'm up to today. Avoiding my own painful death. Why is this not fun?"

When you change it to, *What do I really want?* you might see that what you really want is to have no mortgage payment ever again. You might want the house to be completely paid off so you don't worry about the mortgage every month. And because you are willing to identify it as a want, you might even think of a creative way to do that.

Take some time to notice the difference between needs and wants in your life. You'll start to see the power in switching. For example, sometimes you will do something nice for someone—give them a present, or send them a book or CD just because you like them—and their first response will be, "You didn't need to do that!" And you can say, "Oh, I wanted to!" And that brightens everything up.

You can practice this. You can sit down with a piece of paper and draw a line down the middle. You can write your needs down on the left side of the paper. (Be honest. How many are there really right now?) When you do this exercise, you'll soon find yourself crossing off many items you used to think were needs. Now on the right side, put down your wants. And start to plan your activities based on your wants. It's amazing how many of those wants will come into reality because you've put them down there on paper, you've made them real for yourself, and you've allowed yourself to think about how to bring them into your life.

15. Don't Invent; Reinvent

Success is doing ordinary things extraordinarily well.

Jim Rohn

People are always looking to invent a whiz-bang totally original thing that the world has never seen before. And that's going to make them rich. But most of the wealth that's been created in the world comes from *reinvention* of an *existing* service or product.

When the Japanese made the jump from being a war-torn nation to being a real industrial power, it was by rein-venting things that were already invented. All they did was improve on products that were already out there on the marketplace.

They didn't have to invent the automobile.

Creativity itself is more reinvention than invention. It's the art of combining existing elements. Most people think creativity is the magical production of something out of nothing. It's not. Mozart said, "I never wrote an original melody in my life." He re-combined old folk melodies that he heard in his youth, and that's where he came up with his music.

When Steve started out as a public speaker some 15 years ago, he tried to be just a motivational speaker like everyone else. He thought of Tom Hopkins, Zig Ziglar, Jim Rohn, and Tony Robbins when he took the stage. And he was okay, but his business was just not really taking off.

But he also had a love of acting and stand-up comedy, too, which he thought of as totally separate and unrelated fields. But then one day he decided on the spot to combine all three fields into one chaotic performance. He brought alarming stories of his own failures in life into the motivational speeches in a funny way that caught audiences by surprise. He no longer stayed inside a safe paradigm called "motivational speaker." He replaced it with something wilder and more personally risky. He re-combined and reinvented the job.

Soon he was combining the elements of stand-up comedy with elements of strong motivation and pathetic personally confessional monologues. All of a sudden people were saying, "That guy's a true original. We've got to hire that guy again. Nobody's like him."

"I loved it that people thought that I was the ultimate original," Steve recalls. "But I was actually combining Sam Kinison, Leo Buscaglia, Louie Anderson, Tom Peters, and Spalding Gray. Rather than being truly original, I just combined a number of elements that hadn't been in this field before."

When Sam started his music and dance studios, he would walk through the competition's sites, just to get a feel for what he was up against. In these competing studios, he saw clearly that those people did not care. The furniture was rough and tattered, the carpets needed to be replaced, and in one, even the sign was broken outside. They just didn't care.

So Sam knew that he didn't have to invent a new way to run a studio. All he had to do was reinvent the original idea, but this time with obsessive *caring* for the customer.

"I walked into an auto parts store the other day," Steve said, "and even though there were four guys there behind the counter, not one guy even looked up at me. And the store was empty. I had to clear my throat and make a little fuss of myself just to get noticed. It was like walking into San Quentin. Not that I know what that's like."

Those people behind the counter *were* in a prison. They were locked down in their own minds. Their brains held them inside a depressed, pessimistic view of the world of work. It wouldn't take much to take all their business away! You wouldn't have to invent anything. You'd just have to inject some caring into the matrix. Like the old Chinese proverb says, "A man without a smile should not open a shop."

You can do this with anything. Creativity is about energetic re-combinations. It's not about wondering if you're a true original. It's better to be a genuine fake than a true original!

Even if you were to open up a steakhouse across the street from a steakhouse, all you'd have to do is be better than they are at everything. And all of a sudden they'd have no business and you'd have all the business.

So reinventing is just having the enthusiasm to do an extraordinary job, which is lacking in so many careers and businesses right now. That alone will set you apart.

How many businesses do you walk into every day where there is no evidence anywhere that anyone wants to do a good job? We experience that every day. So to "reinvent" a service offered to the public, all you have to do is really be conscious of what other people *aren't* doing.

16. Learn from the Richest Guy in the Bible

Great men are they who see that spiritual is stronger than any material force; that thoughts rule the world.

Ralph Waldo Emerson

The richest guy in the Bible was King Solomon.

In the ancient scriptures God visits the newly crowned Solomon in a dream and offers him anything he pleases. Solomon asks for "an understanding heart." Pleased with his non-greedy wish, God tells Solomon that not only will he receive greater intellect and wisdom than any other man who will ever live, but also great wealth, "which thou hast not asked, both riches and honor: so that there shall not be any among the kings like unto thee all thy days."

The lesson was that it's the wisdom (not the money) that is rewarded. It's the understanding heart that leads to wealth, not the other way around.

Most people want money so that they can finally have inner peace in their hearts. Their hearts are troubled by all things related to money. They argue with their loved ones about money. Money makes them crazy with anxiety.

They haven't learned the ancient lesson from the story

of Solomon. Wisdom first, money second. An understanding heart receives more wealth than a worried mind.

When you imagine creating wealth you may imagine that money is the best thing you get from your efforts, but it's not so. It's really the knowledge and the wisdom that you acquire along the way.

"If I had to choose between giving up all my possessions or giving up the knowledge I've acquired up to this point, I would keep the knowledge," Sam says. "It's far more valuable."

You can always re-create what you have materially. When Japan and Germany were reduced to rubble in World War II, they re-created everything and became world economic powers. Study wealthy people over time who have made fortunes and lost fortunes and made the fortunes back, and you start to realize that the knowledge is the real asset. People who exceed their financial goals consistently say that reaching the goal wasn't the payoff. It was *who they became* along the way.

It's never what you get. It's who you become.

The same will be true with you. As you highlight the ideas in this book that click with you and apply them to your own opportunities in life, you will create wealth. And we are basing that prediction on the fact that our individual coaching clients, who now number in the hundreds, and who come from all walks of life and temporary failure, use these very thinking tools to create wealth for themselves. And yet in the end it's not the wealth they love most. It's the knowledge and wisdom they have acquired. It's the *ability* they now have.

So even if a catastrophe wiped their material wealth out and they had to start over, they know they could do it. And would do it.

17. Read Your Fan Mail

The higher your self-esteem, the more likely it is that you will
be innovative rather than ritualistic and tradition-bound in your
work. This ensures greater success in a world of increasingly
rapid change.

Nathaniel Branden

One of the deadliest wealth-killers is lack of self-esteem.
The low self-esteem way to start the day is: "I'm not worth
it. Who would ever want to hire me? Why would they want
to promote me? Should I even apply for that leadership
position?"

This lack of self-esteem offers no traction at all.

When you lose confidence in the value of what you
have to offer, it gets harder and harder to ask for it. Because
people ultimately pay you—not what they think you're
worth—but what *you think you're worth*.

Exchanging money is always an exchange of energy.
Sometimes it's just the energy of thought, but it's still energy. And it's hard to bring that energy up from a place of
low self-worth. So one of the best ways to keep your confidence and your sense of value high is to read your fan mail.

Any time you get an email complimenting your work,
save it. Save it to a certain file. Save all of the rave reviews

for anything you do to a certain file. Keep a little journal or notebook. If somebody calls and thanks you or compliments you, jot it down. Because there's going to be a time in your week next week or next month, where, before you go to a very important meeting, you're going to want to read through those notes and really get who you are.

We let our self-esteem slip by not paying attention to it. And sometimes it takes another person to come in and boost us and remind us how good we are. Sometimes our partner or our spouse plays that role and pumps us up before we have a big, important conversation. But don't rely on it. Better to be in charge of that function yourself. After all, it is called *self*-esteem.

18. Stop Mowing Your Lawn

If you don't know what to do with many of the papers on
your desk, stick a dozen colleagues' initials on them and
pass them along. When in doubt, route.

Malcolm Forbes

Get someone else to mow your lawn. Get someone else
to buy your paper clips. Get someone else to do the smaller time-consuming jobs that keep you from your best
thinking.

When we coach people we make recommendations for
actions that we know will change their prosperity. But sometimes they hesitate. They say they have no time! They don't
know where to fit transformation into a life that is so busy.

"I haven't mowed my own lawn for probably seven
years now," Sam says. "I actually do own a lawn mower so
I don't look like, you know, too much of a person who's
above that—but I think I've used it twice and each time I
said, 'This is crazy!'"

Sam says he's keeping things around the house like
lawnmowers and tools as props for his kids so they
don't get the wrong idea. He doesn't want them to give

interviews later in life and say, "We never saw a lawn mower around the house."

"Eventually I'm going to have to get an empty briefcase and dress up in a suit and leave the house once in a while. Just so they're not living in this bizarre fantasy world."

We're not saying never do anything with your hands. In fact, some people get great satisfaction and relaxation from yard work. It's a full Zen retreat for them on weekends to work in the yard. But they are doing it mindfully, joyfully for that very reason. Not because it's a part of their stressful life of things that "need to get done."

One CEO we were coaching was late for his meeting with 200 people because he was out buying office supplies for his company. Paper clips! He had gotten so involved in doing all these little things that he had lost his bearings. We gave him some daily inquiries to practice: "What are the things that if I did them would be high-return actions?" And, "What are the things that others could do that I could delegate?"

Are you yourself doing a lot of $10-an-hour tasks? Yet you could be having communications that yield 20, 200 or 2,000 times more return than $10. And that's the whole point. Always do the math. Always keep your eye on the big picture and don't get sucked into the quicksand of stressful needy tasks.

The great health guru Andrew Weil says he just loves washing dishes. He always volunteers to do dishes at gatherings. One might think, wait, he's the rich and famous Andrew Weil! He doesn't have to wash dishes. But it's loving it that draws him to it. Loving it. People create wealth in their lives when they love what they are doing. Not when they "need to do" what they're doing.

When Napoleon Hill said, "Think and grow rich" he was really asking people to elevate their consciousness. Stop feeling (stressed) and start thinking (what would I love to do?). He was saying "think" in the same way that IBM used to say "think." In the early days of IBM they used to have the word "think!" all over the walls in their buildings. And what they really meant was "Get out of this non-thinking, low consciousness, habitual, busy work that people hide out in."

Focus on doing what gets you what you want.

19. Be a Complaint Department

Restlessness and discontent are the first necessities of progress.

Thomas Edison

One of the ways we've seen small businesses and individuals turn around to prosperity is in their relationship to complaints.

When people start welcoming complaints and seeing complaints as a door to greater knowledge of the customer, breakthroughs occur. When complaints are seen as possible opportunities, then everything changes.

However, most people don't want to hear complaints. They feel kicked in the stomach by a complaint. Therefore the logical process of creating wealth is replaced by emotional survival.

A store owner named Donnie was a client of ours, and as we waited in the lobby before our meeting with him, we overheard him in his office as he fielded calls about unhappy customers.

"Oh yeah, yeah…he's unhappy about our delivery time…tell him I'll call him back. I don't have time for that today."

Donnie didn't understand the opportunity he was passing up. Complaints threatened him and triggered his most negative emotions.

Donnie was missing out on an opportunity to really learn what his customers wanted. He didn't see that if he engaged his complaints, he would solve his biggest mystery: What are the things my customers really value? That information is gold. When Donnie's not emotional, he knows it's gold because he goes to many long seminars on how to understand customers' hidden needs. The seminars teach him that the road to attracting new customers through referrals comes from understanding the customers you already have. When he goes to those seminars he is being logical, so he takes notes like crazy. But when a real live customer complains, he becomes emotionally defensive all over again. Missing his chance all over again.

Donnie can't see that the customer is going to tell him how to improve his business. He can't see it because the information is disguised as a complaint. Business improvement will be spoken to him, but Donnie won't hear it.

Instead, he gets threatened, gets defensive, and doesn't want to talk to him. There he was, facing someone who had experienced his work intimately, ready to tell him the change he needed to make to take it to the next level, and he didn't want to talk to him!

Another opportunity to mine complaints like gold occurs when people quit the team. Usually when people quit, the owners grieve and get over it. Or else they yell, "Good riddance!" But one of the greatest ways to reduce turnover is to increase the attention that you pay to your exit interviews. Why did this person leave? It could tell you a lot, even if you're glad they left.

People want to isolate themselves from any "bad news." Not realizing that bad news is good when you have a creative mind. A purely creative quest for wealth converts bad news to opportunity.

You can set a new tone starting today that welcomes complaints of any kind. Soon your people realize that you're not going to flip out, melt down, or freak out if you hear about something that isn't going great. You're going to be grateful for it. When you set that tone, then complaints will be brought to you sooner and success will move forward all the faster.

Lance Secretan, the founder of Manpower, Inc., said, "What would happen if we looked at a customer and saw the face of God in them? To most people it sounds like a lofty idea. But—if you see the face of God in a flower, why wouldn't you see it in the face of a customer?"

20. Take a Step Away

If there is any one secret of success, it lies in the ability to get the other person's point of view and see things from that person's angle as well as from your own.

Henry Ford

What service do you currently deliver? Anyone with a profession has one. What's the process for delivering your service? Can you take a step out of that process?

Because one of the ways you can really start to make money is to remove a step from your current process.

For example, Netflix took the step of going to the video store away. You no longer have to drive to the store to get a video or DVD or drive back to avoid late charges. That step is gone. They created huge immediate wealth by removing that step.

To find these steps that might be removed, ask yourself "What do my clients or customers have to do to receive my service? What process am I forcing them to do that could be eliminated?"

If you can take any step out of the process they will be delighted, because as so many social observers have noted, "Time is the new money." If you can simplify things for people and make it easier for them to save time, they will reward you with money.

Steve used to set tables up in the back of the room at a place where he was speaking where people could come back at breaks or after the speech to buy his books. Now the books are built into the speaking contract so that they are already on people's chairs when they arrive to hear him. Step removed.

There's a bank here that we go to that has removed a step. It used to be that when you went into the bank, the thing you really didn't look forward to was waiting in line. Just to see a teller merely to make a deposit. This bank has taken that step out! If they see someone waiting in line, they have one of their people walk up and say, "Are you making a deposit? If you are, I can take your deposit right now." They take it, they fill out the form, and we walk away not having to wait in line. So they have taken that waiting in line step out of the process. Because of that, we just rave about this bank, and some friends and relatives have already switched over to them. More wealth for the bank.

No matter what service or product you deliver to any-one, even in a large organization, just ask yourself, "Does it have to be done this way? Can I save someone some time here? Can I take a step away?"

Think of the music industry. You can download music now. The step of going to the record store was taken away.

A lot of times you can just look over what your cus-tomers are going through. All the forms they are filling out. Whatever it is, whatever you are making them do, ask yourself, "Do they have to really do all that? Do we really need that from them? Is there a way we can bypass that for them?" Keep asking that question.

As Jack Welch has said, "Speed is everything. It is the indispensable ingredient of competitiveness. Speed, sim-plicity, and self-confidence are closely intertwined."

At one time, you could just read books, but then when audio books came along, a whole new industry was created by the ability to have something recorded so you could listen to it, as opposed to just reading it. Soon eBooks came along and you could just download a book. Then music downloads happened.

So if you're selling something today, you don't have to improve the product itself to accelerate your wealth. You can simply improve how it's delivered. How do you deliver what you do? Could it be done faster? Could you make it more convenient for the recipient of your work?

And you don't have to be an entrepreneur with a business to make these ways drive your success curve. Even working from a cubicle in a bureaucracy, you can revolutionize the delivery of your own work (take a step away) and win a promotion from having done so.

21. Become Surprising

The best kept secret in the global economy today is this: When your service is awesome you get so stinking rich you have to buy new bags to carry all the money home.

Tom Peters

To become a legend for who you are and what your business is, the secret is to surprise people. You can't do it by just being good at what you do. Nobody walks around spreading the urban legend that you are just good at what you do. That's a boring thing to say. And boring statements evaporate, never to be repeated. They don't survive as stories.

The true objective is to achieve what our good friend Darby Checketts refers to as "Customer Astonishment." It's the way you can really generate word of mouth and legendary status.

Like Jesus did when he raised Lazarus from the dead. People's jaws dropped, and the story won't stop circulating.

Look for that element of surprise. Go the extra mile and do the unexpected. In everything related to service.

So if somebody asks for one thing, you do just a little bit more than they ask for. Or you do it faster than they would have expected. Or any little touch that surprises.

Because it's the element of surprise that works. It's a powerful military strategy to use the element of surprise, but it's also a tremendous wealth creation strategy.

Nordstrom became a legend by startling customers. They became absurd! They were outrageous in how they served customers. One lady was worried that she couldn't get her new dress altered in time for a big party on the east coast, and she had to catch a plane the next day. And when she got to the east coast, she found the dress waiting for her in the hotel room with a ribbon around it and a box of chocolates, and "Thanks for using Nordstrom."

Nordstrom would go way out of its way to absolutely startle and astonish its customers. Out of those single acts, people talked. Surprise someone enough and they'll talk forever. People talked about Nordstrom everywhere they went, which was worth hundreds of thousands of dollars in advertising. Urban legends popped up. Soon we didn't know which stories about Nordstrom were true.

And so you, too, can generate outrageous word of mouth if you allow yourself to be outrageous whenever you have the chance.

Most people operate in terms of customer satisfaction. They just walk around wondering whether their customers are satisfied or not. But the problem with customer satisfaction is that customers *expect* to be satisfied. Therefore customer satisfaction does not create wealth.

A "satisfied" customer never speaks to others about you. She never gets any buzz going about what you offer, because she is merely satisfied.

When we were in school and got a grade that was "satisfactory," that was a "C". C equals satisfactory, and nobody raved or celebrated a kid getting a C in anything because it was just average. It was barely getting by.

Yet, most people still look at their customers with the question of whether they are satisfied or not. While one of the quickest ways to wealth is to ask a different question.

It's a question we first heard asked by Darby Checketts (who has appeared at our seminars) when he said, "Are you willing to astonish your customers?" Darby has since written a book called *Customer Astonishment*, and we recommend it highly.

Don't worry if it borders on the absurd to make "customer astonishment" your standard. You'll get used to living out there on the edge. Soon you will look forward to making your mind stretch by answering the question: "What could I do right now that would astonish my customer?" You are automatically thinking out of the box. You are pushing the limits of your imagination, and you're coming up with things you never came up with when you lived inside the dim world of customer satisfaction.

The great car dealer Carl Sewell said, "If we treat a guy well, he'll buy a lot of cars from us over time and tell at least one friend. At $35,000 a pop that could easily add up to a half million bucks. I tell everyone from the reception desk to the service bay, that guy is a $500,000 bill walking in the store, ready to be won over, if we all work together to make him our best friend."

One of the things that happens with an astonished customer is that he talks and talks and talks. Word of mouth has always been the best advertising for any of us. And word of mouth comes from people who are surprised by something. Any time anything surprises you, that's what you talk about! And so the really great creative game is to get your people together to continuously ask the question "What can we do that would astonish people?"

You don't have to be a company to do this. You can do this yourself as an individual. How can you astonish someone who means a lot to you? Astonish! Not just please and satisfy. It opens up the brain to think in weird ways, and it inspires amazing, unforgettable actions.

22. Look Inside Your Heart

What's love got to do with it?

Tina Turner

Hall of Fame pro quarterback Fran Tarkenton has always said, "If it's not fun, you're not doing it right."

A great motto for wealth creation.

There's something about getting what you love to do in alignment with what you're really doing that's going to create wealth in your life faster. When you're doing something that's really fun for you, you're able to do it without watching the clock.

Anything you do in that timeless state is "your thing" as they used to say. It's your passion, and the advantage to you is that you do it tirelessly with a mind open to continuous innovation. The work is not a burden and it doesn't really feel like work. So you're more creative with it and you've got higher energy for it.

Many people watched TV and decided that real estate, with no money down, was the way to get money. But if they had no real love of real estate, then all the tasks they did were done in dreary linear time. They would always be watching the clock. Tick tock. They would not be in that zone where energy gets high, intuition soars, and they're making all the right moves. That would never happen. Instead they were finding real estate to be absolute drudgery. They had no heart for it.

Steve spent a lot of time long ago working in the world of advertising and marketing because he thought there was money there, although he didn't really love it. People always told him that if you can write, and be expressive and creative, the only way to make money in this society is to go into advertising. He went into it and he did all right, but he didn't really love it. So when he was in an agency that finally failed badly, he took a long walk and looked into his heart and looked back over his life.

Steve recalls, "I thought, 'OK I don't know what work I'm going to do next, so why don't I just take a minute and find out what would I really love to do?"

He couldn't think of what that was. So he took more time with it and thought, "Well, when have I been really, really happy? When have I really felt joy doing something?" And then he remembered some talks he had given way back in the early days when he was recovering from an addiction and was in some 12-step programs where you would get up in front of the room and talk to groups of people about your recovery.

Steve recalled, "That was the most fun and the most thrilling and the most enjoyable time of my life to talk to a whole room full of people. So I thought, 'OK, well, that's a sign that maybe that's what I should be doing for a living.' So I started to look around and I remembered a guy who gave a talk to an advertising client of mine and I thought I'd look him up and partner up with him to see if I could do what he does for a living."

That man's name was Dennis Deaton. He was a seminar leader and a public speaker, and Steve went to work for him just to apprentice with him to find out how he did it. Soon he was doing speeches himself and talking to rooms full of people, loving it, and doing it more and more.

Steve said, "True wealth didn't come into my life until I started doing what I loved. I also knew that I loved writing, too, so I started writing books connected with my speaking, and more success then started to come indirectly from that."

So don't think it's selfish to do what you want to do. Your happiness is a wealth-attractor. Not the other way around. Most people have it the other way around: I'll allow myself to be happy when I make enough money. When I pay my debts. When I have a house. When I have a second home. When I have a boat, a new spouse, etc., into futile insanity.

Reverse that. Do what you love, and the money will follow.

Another aspect of this principle is to find ways to work with people you love working with.

"I don't want to get too corny," Sam says, "but I always say that the business I have with my wife is the business that love built. It really is because I just love working with my wife, and I love that I am able to do the things to actually be with my family. I think people have to switch away from thinking it's either one or the other—you either have a great business that makes a lot of money or you have a family life. You can have both."

So if you are starting to wonder how to create wealth in your life, take time to be alone, take a long walk, take a hot bath, rent a cabin (stay there for a weekend with no TV or entertainment and just be with yourself). Relax your brain and listen to your heart. It's very important to gravitate toward what you love to do, because anything you love to do is going to create wealth faster than trying to do something you think you *should* do or something that someone told you was a hot new opportunity.

Mark Twain once said, "The law of work does seem utterly unfair—but there it is, and nothing can change it; the higher the pay in enjoyment the worker gets out of it, the higher shall be his pay in money also."

23. Get Up on the Barstool

Simplicity is the ultimate sophistication.

Leonardo DaVinci

Steve used to refer to this as his "bar stool test." ("Until I quit drinking, fortunately. Then I began calling it the 'elevator speech'—what you would say if you met someone in an elevator.")

The bar stool test was based on you sitting on a bar stool next to some other person who says, "What do you do?" And now you've got 10 seconds to answer the question.

It's really important to be able to describe in 10 seconds or less to a complete stranger what it is you offer. What's unique about it?

You must have a very exciting way of describing what you do. If you lead a team, it helps when all your people know this short description. Then your people on the phone can say it quickly.

What do you do? What separates you? What makes you different? You'll be able to state very quickly what your advantage is and why people love your work and why they would want to use your service—why they would want to pay a great deal of money for it.

The advantage of keeping your story sweet and simple is that it gets to spread much faster. You actually teach other people to talk about you in this way—in a very simple way—so when they go talk to other people, they can remember it.

One of the best examples of this occurred years ago when restaurants did not deliver pizza, and Domino's decided to deliver pizzas to your door. Believe it or not, to get a pizza you used to have to get in your car and go for it, or make it at home! And Domino's had a new slogan that just said "Domino's Pizza Delivers." That was their whole ad campaign! That was their mission statement, their business plan, their unique selling proposition, and their branding all spoken in three words! Domino's Pizza delivers. It was so simple that everybody could remember it. Soon people would repeat it over and over—Domino's Pizza delivers! Whenever there was a party going and someone would say, "Let's go get some pizza," someone else would immediately sing "Domino's Pizza delivers!" And they would call Domino's and get their pizza delivered.

Steve remembers, "When I started as a public speaker, I wanted to have something like that that was short and simple that would separate me from the rest. I was waiting until somebody who saw me speak could say it precisely, and I kind of coached it and teased it out of him until he said what I wanted, and then I used his quote everywhere. It was a quote from my friend Fred Knipe who was an Emmy award-winning TV screen writer, and when he saw me speak he said, 'Steve Chandler's an insane combination of Jerry Seinfeld and Anthony Robbins.' Ever since he said that, everybody has been using that quote. Everybody would tell their people that's who I was. People who introduced me would say that. People who wanted to see if they wanted to have me come and speak would put that quote on the top of any e-mail that said, 'We're thinking about using this guy,' and that just sort of became my thing and that was my barstool talk—it was my one thing. Of course I had to live up to it, but at the same time it described who I was compared to the other speakers."

So it's really important that you get a simple, short expression in your own mind of what it is you are offering in exchange for wealth. Something people can remember and repeat. When you get it crystallized and into 10 seconds, it will pay off for you.

24. Learn From the Dolphin Trainers

There is more hunger for love and appreciation in this world than for bread.

Mother Teresa

You can get more accomplished by being positive with people than being negative. We've always heard that "the squeaky wheel gets the oil" and you have to raise your voice and complain to get anything done, but the truth is if you are a real pain to deal with, you'll get sabotaged in ways you'll never even know about.

Sam says, "I only like working with customers I actually like. If people make too many foolish demands on me, you know they go to the bottom of the list. My saying is actually this, 'The squeaky wheel gets taken off and replaced with a wheel that doesn't squeak.'"

Dolphin trainers have figured out that if you give the dolphins a tiny fish for jumping through the hoop, the dolphin will jump through the hoop again.

The trainers don't take a baseball bat and beat the dolphin for not jumping through the hoop.

Animal trainers have learned over the years that positive reinforcement is the most efficient training tool in the world. And it's even more true with humans.

We were once called into a little law firm that was bringing us on as consultants to help them get more referral business. In the first meeting Steve said to the lawyers sitting around the table, "Let's start here. How do you reward the referrals you get right now?" Total silence. Steve then said, "Let's go around the table and you can each tell me how you do that." They had nothing to say. One lawyer said it would be unethical.

Soon we had put referral-tracking systems in place where someone referring a client would be thanked sincerely in many ways from many people in the firm. Not only that, but when the case had a successful outcome, the lawyer who referred the client would get a full briefing on how things turned out, with another series of thanks for contributing to such a successful outcome. Referrals more than doubled in the first year.

Whatever it is you want more of, inside whatever system you are using to create wealth, ask yourself the question, "How do I reward it now?" In business or any enterprise, you get what you reward.

If you are interacting with vendors, employees, customers, partners, or even supervisors, positive reinforcement for them is powerful, as opposed to criticizing how they serve you. Positive reinforcement and appreciation go a long way to getting better service, better prices, and more referrals.

If you work just by yourself and you rely on quick printers and small businesses that you outsource part of your business to, positive reinforcement holds the same power. Your world is full of dolphins who will jump through hoops for you. So do like the dolphin trainers do, and people will serve you better and better and put you at the top of their list. They love hearing how they've helped you.

The negative feedback approach is what most people do. They expect good service, and when they don't get it they complain loudly. But they don't realize that the people they complained to will now put them at the bottom of their preferred customer list—subtly, even subconsciously—because most people are negative about complaints.

Positive reinforcement works with all species. All God's creatures respond to positive reinforcement much faster than negative feedback, and yet we forget to do it. However, the more we remember to integrate it into whatever it is we are doing to create wealth, the faster the wealth comes toward us.

25. Let People In with the In Crowd

There is only one boss: the customer. And he can fire everybody
in the company, from the chairman on down, simply by
spending his money somewhere else.

Sam Walton

One of the best ways to create wealth is to look for ways
you can have an inner circle of exclusivity. If you're doing
a special introductory evening, don't have it be open to all
comers; have it be open to a certain number. If more want
to come, put them on a waiting list for the next time.

Anytime you can really become exclusive, you increase
the word of mouth. People talk about you. Harley
Davidson stumbled into this when they ran short of product at one point and people had to go on a waiting list to
buy a motorcycle. The company was worried that it would
turn customers off, but the opposite happened. It increased
the desire for Harley Davidsons. It made them look like
marketing geniuses! So they kept the policy in. Now everyone waits his turn.

You can do the same. You can look for ways for exclusivity and limitation and be real about it so that it increases

your ability to make money. People want to be a part of a special inside group.

You will be using the law of supply and demand to your advantage. It's basic economics. When the supply of something decreases and demand increases, the price can naturally go up.

That's why single-family houses in fast-growing areas increase in price. With less supply in the market and more demand from buyers, the price naturally increases. So if you can use this in your business and create a real supply and demand scenario where you have limited supply and more demand, you will prosper. You don't have to always have more than enough for everyone.

Sometimes our coaching clients say, "It's unfair if I don't have enough for every single customer!"

But think about it. You can't anyway. There are a lot more customers in your market area than you can have enough supply for. So you might as well use that fact to your advantage and really strengthen your pricing. You can afford to increase your price, and you can afford to do the other extra kind of things to make the actual service that you are doing a lot more valuable to people.

Most people don't see the value of putting a limit on what they offer. Their sense of greed and need are too great.

We have a client we will call Suzanne who was putting on her quarterly seminar on fitness. She had 75 people signed up, and we asked her how many people she wanted to attend the event.

"Well, wow, we *could* put 200 in there."

"Yeah, but what is reasonable…."

"We could get around 110, maybe 115."

"Great, so why not limit the attendance to 100? Don't let anybody come in over 100. Let everybody know you've got 25 seats left and that's it."

"No, no, no, we can get 105! I don't want to turn away that money. I need it. I need it. God knows I need it."

Suzanne couldn't yet see that limitation would create value. If she limited the seating, people would want to ensure their seats faster and she could eventually charge more per seat and spend less on advertising because the best advertising slogan of all time is "SOLD OUT!"

If she limited seating to 100 and sold out quickly, she would have even more success selling her next event because she could tell people, "Now the last one was sold out and we had to turn people away. Those people were put on a waiting list so they are coming to this one. Would you like to come to this one?" And people would sign up immediately!

Most people don't understand limitation. They don't see that it creates value. They think somehow they should always vacuum up every penny from every straggler and always fit them in. Anybody with money is welcome always because our need is so great.

Sam's studio business was the first one in his area to say "We're only going to put six kids in a three-year-old class, and we're only going to put 12 kids in a class of nine-year-olds." At the time there were competing studios that put 18, 20 or 26 in a class because they were always willing to cram the extra people in there for the money. They needed the money so badly.

But wealth and success don't come from desperation. Customers tend to want what they can't have. They value it more. Limitation creates a burning desire in your customer base that wasn't there before. Everything shifts. You don't need to vacuum in that extra dollar today. You want to be successful long-term.

When the Cleveland Indians built their new ballpark, they built it smaller than the older one. People said, "Wait, you're nuts" because the population's bigger than before. The fan base is larger! They just couldn't understand how limitation increased the value. And once Cleveland started selling out their games, people bought future games like crazy. And the players probably played better, too. In front of a packed house instead of those depressing half-empty ballparks. Everything was better.

Dictate the limitation. Limit your availability and you will make your potential unlimited.

26. Cut Players from the Team

It's not the people you fire who make your life miserable
... it's the people you don't fire who make your life miserable.

Harvey Mackay

Tom Peters is a business guru and former McKinsey consultant whose many books and lectures have done more to transform top American businesses than any other individual's in the past 20 years.

(We go to his website every week and always learn something valuable at www.tompeters.com.)

Peters recently posted a formula on his website for making a business, or any team, truly great. We were delighted to see this formula, because it matched up exactly with our own experience of working with leaders and teams over the past years. This formula works. And it's so simple, it might not be taken seriously. In fact, it's so simple it almost embarrasses us to put it here. But here goes. One promise: follow the formula and your numbers will jump through the roof; our experience proves it.

The Way to Succeed:
HIRE SUNNY! FIRE GLOOMY!
Hire/Promote those with....Sunny Dispositions.
Fire those with perpetually...Gloomy Dispositions.
(Hint: The farther up the Organization you go,
the more important this gets.)
(Rule: Leaders are not permitted to have "bad days"....
especially on Bad Days!)
(Rule: One Sad Dog can infect a group of 100.)
(Rule: One Energetic, Optimistic, Sunny Soul
can motivate an army to move a mountain.)

If you are in a professional relationship with someone who is not in harmony with the rest of the team or with your own values or commitment to success, don't hesitate even for a second to end that relationship. Remember, you didn't take vows. This isn't about "loyalty." It's about success.

We coach a lot of business owners who are afraid to let a toxic person go. They are afraid they don't have anyone to replace that person with.

Like Tom Peters says, "fire gloomy" and deal with the fear instead of continuing to deal with that person. You'll be happy you did.

In all our years of coaching we've never known anyone who regretted firing a gloomy person. However, we know countless people who regretted keeping those people on too long. They all wish they had acted sooner.

Even for the sake of the other person! You are setting them free from an unhappy work situation. You can tell them that they are the "right person in the wrong job" and you're going to help them find the right job. You'll be amazed at how many people take the firing as a badly-needed wake-up call and turn their professional lives around afterward. Give that gift to your difficult person today. You'll be glad you did.

27. Love Your Enemy

Competition is not only the basis of protection to the consumer,
but it is the incentive to progress.

Herbert Hoover

The brilliant marketing consultant Jay Abraham has
transformed hundreds of businesses in his lifetime, including our own. He says, "When it comes to your life or business it really comes down to 'Grow or Die.'"

This is an extremely powerful, but frequently over-
looked, concept. Even if you are somewhat satisfied with
your life or business progress, you cannot stagnate, if you
want to keep on living and thriving. And competition
forces you to grow. (Or die.)

The great business analyst Peter Drucker said, "Either
you work hard to make obsolete and replace or improve
your current business model, product or service—or your
competition will do it for you—and to you."

This is even more true in personal life, where openness
to growth, openness to finding new levels of energy, and
openness to more intelligent goals is vital to happiness and
life itself. In human success, as in nature: if you stop something from growing, you will kill it.

Your competitors therefore must not be seen as a bad thing. They are not! They are here to inspire your own growth and enlightenment.

Most people see competition as trouble. But your competitors can be your greatest teachers.

First of all, they will make mistakes for you that you can learn from! So watch them closely. They can also do new things that you can also learn and grow from. You can take their best (non-protected) practices and make them your own.

And appreciate also that they can advertise for you. Most competitors don't know how to do highly-targeted direct-response advertising, so they will advertise in such a way that people will respond to the general idea, not a particular company. Their ads will have people come to them and come to you, too!

You can also study versions of competitors in other cities. As you visit other cities, other cities' newspapers, other cities' yellow pages, even on the internet, start looking at the communications of your competitors. They will teach you a great deal.

In your study, it is important to keep your intention focused on releasing all negative feelings about competition. Competition has always made people better, not worse at what they do.

Even internal competition! One of the best things you can do to a sales staff, in our experience as sales trainers and coaches, is to bring in a brand new sales super star. Add her to the staff and let her become the number one salesperson. Watch what happens. Everyone else gets better.

Therefore, competition is always good. It's never the reason you are having a hard time attracting wealth. Although many people think it's the primary reason they are having trouble.

Wayne Calloway, the chairman of PepsiCo from 1986 – 96, said, "Nothing focuses the mind better than the constant sight of a competitor who wants to wipe you off the map."

The fact that you have competitors means that your business is an attractive industry that has enough interest to sustain multiple operators. If you are the only one in a new industry and no one has ever heard of the service that you are providing, you have a monumental job of educating consumers to why you exist and why they should use you. Your competitors can do a lot of that work for you.

Customers don't care if your good service ideas are original or borrowed. They just want to be served the best way they can.

Success is a logical process, and the only time it goes south and gets off the track is when emotions creep in. And one of the most destructive and unnecessary emotions is to think fearful things about your competitors. To let them scare you.

Competition gets a game going. When people play games it awakens them to a higher level of performance rather than just going to work every day. Competition gets a spirited element introduced into your work—how can we beat them? How can we offer something better? It can be viewed as fun and not a threat.

When you hear a competitor is moving in, the best response is, "Bring them on!"

28. Deliver Experience

Wealth, like happiness, is never attained
when sought after directly.
It comes as a by-product of providing a useful service.

Henry Ford

One of the first things we do with our clients is to get them to stop advertising and making big claims about themselves. Stop networking. Stop schmoozing. Stop "getting your name out."

No one was ever moved to tears by a brochure.

Most people, by wanting to get their name out there, put way too many costly, time-wasting, unnecessary steps into the sales process. Instead, give your prospective customer an *experience* of how good you are.

Back in the 1940s vacuum cleaner sales people (the ones who were really successful) would go inside a home in the suburbs and actually throw some awful dirt on the rug. There they were sitting in the living room with the woman of the house, and they had just thrown dirt on the rug! The woman would jump up and say, "Oh, no, I can't believe you did that!" and the sales person would say, "I'll bet you think I will not be able to get this up."

Then he would go to his car and bring in his vacuum cleaner and clean the rug…making it cleaner than ever! The *experience* of having that machine actually clean something on her carpet made that customer really want to have that product. She has now *experienced* how good it is.

Anytime you can do more than just claim things—do more than just hand brochures or CDs or DVDs to people, you can create wealth faster. Look for ways you can deliver the experience of what it is that you have. That way they will come back for more! And you want them coming back for more.

One of the reasons, for example, we don't ever go to certain restaurants is because we haven't been to those restaurants before! People do things they are comfortable doing—they do things they have successfully done before.

There are people who go to grocery stores that don't even have the best prices because they're comfortable with the experience of going there. They might not even have the best service but they have comfort. They've gone there so many times it feels like their personal store.

It is important to learn ways to give people that feeling, and it can only come from experience; it can't come from an email or a brochure.

Notice how many restaurants and little businesses sit empty much of the time. The same is true with individuals at home offices who offer a service. Just sitting there with no business. Hoping their email attack works. Hoping the new website draws people.

The reason people are not doing business with them is because they haven't done it before! It's as if the owner is paralyzed with this paradox. How do I get repeat business from people who have not done business with me? (We wrote an entire book about how to solve this paradox called *The Small Business Millionaire*.)

Because you really can do something. There are countless ways that you can get people to experience who you are. And a lot of it has to do with having a generous, open hand. You've got to open your hand and give a little bit up front so people can experience *what it is* that you are offering and love it and come back for more.

The best seminar we've ever attended in the personal growth field is Byron Katie's nine-day School for the Work. It cost a few thousand to attend, and it was worth every penny because of her brilliantly transformative guidance. And the most amazing thing about Katie is that you can get everything from her for free if you want to. Her two websites, theWork.com and ByronKatie.com, allow you to download audios, videos, interviews, worksheets, articles, and more of her "treasure" than you'd have time to take in during a single day. She gives it all away up front. The result? Do the math: over 300 people paid around $3,000 each for the school we attended. That's wealth creation at its best. And the people were there because of how much of Katie they had *already experienced*.

People think if you give it away you can't charge for it. Absolutely not true. The opposite is true.

Often when we talk to our clients about giving money-back guarantees, they get afraid to do even that. Even though it would cause people to come more confidently to experience their service.

"I've been doing money-back guarantees in our business for almost 10 years now," Sam says, "and I never regretted it. You've got to think in the way of the open hand. People aren't going to take advantage and abuse you—that's fear-based thinking—you know, 'give them an inch and they'll take a mile!' If you're willing to really put yourself out there and say, 'We're so good that we will just refund your money if you're not happy,' people will love you for that. Most of our competitors don't do that— they're just too afraid."

When people don't create wealth it's usually because their fear is blocking it from coming in. One of the mental blocks people put up is the block about the personality and character of their customers. We hear people talk all the time about untrustworthy customers! They dwell on how they really don't like them. But what they've really done is taken their own self-loathing and projected it out onto the customer, which creates a nightmare. Going into business works better when it's not a nightmare.

There's only one way to have wealth really flow to you and that is to love your customer and to put your customer's needs ahead of yours. You can assume that your customer is, at the very least, as good-hearted and trustworthy as you are. Why wouldn't she be? Why shouldn't he be? You are a customer when you go out; now why wouldn't that customer just be you?

When Nordstrom decided to love their customers it just shocked the world—all the things they allowed their customers to do as if their customers were trusted friends and family members (which in the end they are.) There's one out of 20 who is confused and will cause you a problem, and look at your family—there's one out of every few family members who are the same.

Be happy to allow prospective customers to fully experience your service. Be happy to give them everything you can. Their experience of you is what sells in the long run. More than any sales or marketing program ever will.

29. Learn to Keep Breathing

I've got to keep breathing.
It'll be my worst business mistake if I don't.

Steve Martin

Success flows faster to open creative minds. The brain that is fed a steady diet of oxygen produces more ideas. People who are in top physical condition have more energy, more creativity, and are in a better state of mind. They are happier and more fun to deal with.

Elizabeth Barrett Browning lived for years as a sickly child and only regained her strength after moving to Italy where she became one of the world's greatest poets. Her final conclusion about life was "He lives most life who breathes most air."

When people fully understand the physical element of their success, it often surprises them. That "time off" they take to walk or work out or play a sport is actually adding to their success rather than postponing it (as most people fear it would).

Bobby Fischer was the only American in recent times to ever become the world chess champion. He beat the great Russian Boris Spassky. He said that the primary reason that he beat Spassky (he and Spassky had skill levels that were very similar) was that he prepared by swimming laps under water.

By doing this, he had a great deal more oxygen going to his brain during the chess match than Spassky. Spassky was a heavy smoker, was overweight, and saw chess as only a mental game—all you use is your brain so why do you have to take care of your body?

When people really understand the power of integrating mind, body, and spirit—all three elements of success—wealth is drawn to them faster.

Matt Furey is perhaps America's best example of using the leverage contained in the mind-body-spirit synergy to create huge amounts of wealth. Matt is an internet information entrepreneur. He's also a world class athlete. He was the first American to ever win the Shuai-chiao kung fu martial arts title in China. He was also a national champion collegiate wrestler and now he helps people of all ages stay fit and make money on the internet (www.mattfurey.com).

"Believe me," says Matt, "when you combine physical activity with mental activity, it is as if you are moving heaven and earth simultaneously. You are pulling the future into the present in order to make the future your reality."

Take care of yourself physically because you will think better. You'll be more open, you'll listen better, and you'll bring more enthusiasm to what you do. The more you work out and take care of yourself, the better your circulation. Your blood is of a different character, so there's more oxygen going to the brain; and whatever your IQ is, the more oxygen you have going to the brain, the more creative thoughts you will have—it's just a biological fact.

Sam recalls that years back he was having some phobia issues. He was just not crazy about small spaces and got claustrophobic in elevators and on planes. He finally got counseling from a wise person who told him, "It is easier to control your body than it is to control your mind." As a result, Sam learned exercises with his body that allowed his mind to just give up and relax, and the phobia disappeared.

We think we've got a job to do all day. We don't have time to work out. We don't have the luxury to be down there at the club working out today—that would be irresponsible. We need to be here in front of the computer, slamming coffee, and fighting frantically to make this career work! Trying to build security. But is security really what you want? What about wealth?

The TV actor Pierce Brosnan recently said he was happy to have lost the security of being James Bond every year. "When you have the security of a TV series like 'Remington Steele' or a franchise like Bond, you can become complacent," he said. "To have the hunger and bite again and to have that desire and need to give a performance, that's a good feeling to have."

Pierce Brosnan could have stayed in a lower gear. He could have ground it out complaining (as so many actors do) about being typecast by previous roles they played. He could have complained about how older actors get dumped from great roles like James Bond. But he shifted up to the level that gave him the most energy and adventure instead.

The shift that takes you up to higher energy and adventure is just like shifting gears in your sports car. You're not putting in a whole new engine; you're just shifting.

This very week our client Robert was at his computer dealing with testy clients and getting more and more down on his work. He knew he needed a shift in perspective, so he got up and took a walk outside. He looked up into a tree at a bird's nest he had noticed when he came into work, and he began whistling until he saw a little bird peek its beak and eyes out of the nest. Robert laughed and walked back inside and took a seat at his computer. He felt better. Much better. When he started answering emails, he did it with a lighter touch, giving out more thoughtful and compassionate replies than earlier in the day.

What had just happened for Robert? It's important to see that Robert shifted his mind, that he *did* something physically to take his perspective on up to a slightly higher level. The physical element is important here. The mind and the body are part of the same organic whole. So if you lift your body up and walk it outside, you are moving the interior of your mind at the same time. You are now breathing differently.

A body shift will facilitate a mind shift.

Even closing your eyes and taking a deep breath can shift your mind. Closing your eyes will more than likely take your brain waves from excitable Beta into a more orderly relaxed Alpha state—especially if you can close your eyes for 20 seconds and picture a peaceful scene. Alpha.

The point here is to know you are in control of your sports car. Some people live their whole lives stuck in low gear, not even realizing they could shift up and out and watch their vehicle *glide*. When we extend the metaphor we realize that most people don't even want to learn to drive a stick shift. They want to stay with their automatic transmission—the car that shifts for you.

So their mind's version of that is to simply buy into permanent lists of what is bad news and what is good news and then just let the shifting be automatic.

Therefore, if you find out "bad news" your automatic transmission just downshifts *for you*. You don't even have to think about it. You hear bad news and you go into a bad mood. Automatic! You now sit at your desk breathing anxiously. You have the shallow, rapid breaths of a frightened puppy.

If Pierce Brosnan had been on automatic he would have been in a bad mood the moment he found out that the studio was going to go with a younger James Bond—or the moment his TV series *Remington Steele* was canceled. Automatic downshift.

But that's not what he did. He shifted *up* instead of down, and now he's gliding into all kinds of interesting movie roles.

This is something you or I can do, too, anytime we choose to. Just be like Robert and walk outside to look at the bird in the tree. Just getting up from the chair, stretching and walking, then going outdoors and breathing the fresher air more deeply and looking up, up into the tree and making that connection with the bird, that eye contact with another living being on the planet—that is shifting!

Mahatma Gandhi said, "The human body is the Universe in miniature. That which cannot be found in the body, is not to be found in the Universe. . . . It follows therefore, that if our knowledge of our own body could be perfect, we would know the Universe."

The body leads the mind. We think it's always the other way around, that the mind leads the body around like an old hound dog. That the mind has to talk the body out of bed every morning. Well, one of the secrets to mind shifting is that you can do it the other way. The body can lead the mind to higher gear. Like Robert's did.

Like yours will today when you go for a long swim or a long walk or play that fast-paced game of racquetball with your friend. Your mind will not (and can not) stay in the same gear after that.

30. Think Like an Entrepreneur

Even if you haven't encountered great success yet, there is no reason you can't bluff a little and act like you have. Confidence is a magnet in the best sense of the word. It will draw people to you and make your daily life. . . and theirs. . . a lot more pleasant.

Donald J. Trump

One of the ways you can think more like wealthy entrepreneurs think is to learn from them. Study them, get fascinated with them, enjoy them, and identify with them.

There are so many wonderful books written by them. Successful people are not shy about giving away their secrets. They're proud of what they've done. They will start Starbucks and then want to share with the whole world how they did it. They'll start McDonalds and then want to tell everybody about it. There are books about how Google became a multi-billion dollar company. Amazon as well.

You can find the pulse and thinking patterns of successful entrepreneurs from magazines you can read online and books you can read in the library. It will cost you nothing to capitalize on the fact that these people are anxious to share their entrepreneurial strategies. They're not secretive about it. They are absolutely thrilled with their success and love sharing it with everybody.

Four out of five businesses fail. And those four people have probably never saturated themselves with the thinking of the great minds. Most people who are trying in vain to attract wealth don't even go there. They don't even access all those wonderful ideas. They just stay stuck. They commiserate with those other four out of five people whose businesses are in the process of going under. Those are the people they gather with over the weekends, rather than continuously accessing successful people via the internet or via the library.

If you break down the actual French word "entrepreneur," it means to "enter and to take." To come in and to take. The wealth of knowledge on the internet and in the library is inviting you to "come in and take" it, too.

Sam says the main difference between who he was in his successful businesses and who he was in his failed businesses was the 700 books he read after his card was turned down in the grocery store. Sam devoured every book on success he could get his hands on because he wanted to leave no stone unturned.

You can do the same. No one is holding you back from taking in all the knowledge you can. It's all there for you!

And once you've digested the thinking of the great entrepreneurs, don't forget to notice that they all took action. Action! Success is a two-step process, achingly simple.

The first step is to decide what you want.

The second step is to *act* on that decision.

The best description of the second step we've ever read was written by Og Mandino in *The Greatest Salesman in the World*, when he said "I will act now. I will act now. I will act now. Henceforth, I will repeat these words each hour, each day, everyday, until the words become as much a habit as my breathing, and the action which follows becomes as instinctive as the blinking of my eyelids. With these words I can condition my mind to perform every action necessary for my success. I will act now. I will repeat these words again and again and again. I will walk where failures fear to walk. I will work when failures seek rest. I will act now for now is all I have. Tomorrow is the day reserved for the labor of the lazy. I am not lazy. Tomorrow is the day when the failure will succeed. I am not a failure. I will act now. Success will not wait. If I delay, success will become wed to another and lost to me forever. This is the time. This is the place. I am the person."

31. Kill the Monster

When you hire people that are smarter than you are,
you prove you are smarter than they are.

R. H. Grant

You have a small team trying to create wealth. Someone
on your team leaves you. You need somebody else quickly
to replace that person. What will you do?

Will you just put an ad in the paper or go to
Monster.com? That would be the normal, commonplace,
traditional response. Everybody does that.

But if you do that, you'll get a normal, commonplace,
traditional mediocre group of applicants to choose from.
(When you know for a fact that even one truly great person
can turn a business around.)

People who hire people in the traditional, normal
ways get normal, traditional, mediocre people through
that route. One of the things that has dramatically
changed the fortune of so many small business clients that
we coach is to get them mentally elevated when it comes
to recruiting and hiring. We get them to be artful, creative,
and masterful with their never-ending, ongoing recruiting campaign, as if people were their most important
asset of all.

So they don't just hire on a needs-based approach. They don't just put an ad in the paper or go to Monster.com to fill a hole in their lineup. That's all reactive—that's all needs-based, and there's nothing in that activity that is creative. If you want to *create* a team of all stars who are going to produce success, then you need to stay ahead of the curve in recruiting.

You can be as innovative and creative in how you recruit as you can in anything else.

You want to find people who will thoroughly enjoy working with you. You never want to hire anyone who looks at the job as a place that one comes to just to get a paycheck. That kind of person will weigh you down toward the baseline of mediocrity that characterizes most teams today.

Why not allow all your business acquaintances in your community to be on the lookout for good people for you? You can help people that you are already connected with to refer people to you. You'll have your clients and vendors alike always referring good people and committed to helping you build an all-star team.

They will admire your commitment to always hire people as good as you are, if not better.

32. Become Contagious

The real source of wealth and capital in this new era is not material things. It is the human mind, the human spirit, the human imagination, and our faith in the future. That's the magic of a free society. Everyone can move forward and prosper because wealth comes from within.

Steve Forbes

Your mood is contagious. Your spirit permeates throughout the people you work with. Do you want them happier, more upbeat, and innovative? It's up to you and the mood you bring.

Perhaps you think your mood is low because of your worries. Realize worrying is dysfunctional. It actually enlarges the problems you're focused on. It's an abuse and a misuse of the human imagination. It's like praying for what you don't want. It serves no valid purpose. It stresses out the people you're around.

And it's completely optional and avoidable. Or as the wise eighth-century scholar Shantideva said: "If you can solve your problem, then what's the need of worrying? If you cannot solve it, then what's the use of worrying?"

If you lead a big team or just one other person, make sure you are really leading. Whether you are a husband-

and-wife business or enterprise, make sure you are really leading. Have your leadership be contagious—it's going to be anyway, so know that it is and have it be *consciously* contagious.

Why not come into your place of work optimistic, full of good news about the business and directions you are going? Why not talk about the good people you're about to bring on and new locations you are scouting? People will pick up on that and start to connect with their own inner-optimist. The happier you are, the more upbeat and happy your people will be and the more happy, carefree, and generous your customer will be.

Customers pick up on the mood of a work place. Customers pick up on the basic psychic energy of any place that they go into, and when that psychic energy is negative and down because the owner himself is full of worries, then wealth is repelled. Customers pick up on it, and they feel a little uncomfortable when they are in there, so they don't want to spend as much time there (or money). Employees are a little more anxious. Because of the viral downer mood that permeates the place, they soon fantasize about working somewhere else. Soon the owner has to hire someone new and the stress only increases.

So it's important to feel how you want others to feel. If you want employees and customers to be relaxed, happy, and giving, then be that. And if you can't be that, don't come into work. Go do your walk by the lake with your little dog, and enjoy yourself until you get up to the proper level of life enjoyment, and *then* walk into your place of work and be the happy person who arrives at 9:30 a.m. instead of the upset person who comes in at 7:30 spreading bad vibes.

We worked with a business owner named Merv who thought he scored points with everybody in his office because he was always arriving earlier than they were. He wanted the mood and theme to be self-sacrifice. Merv got in early so he could get a jump on all the problems he wanted to worry about. Wealth stayed away from Merv—until he learned to relax.

If you are upbeat, it will lead your people in the contagious way that is described in John Hersey's *Creating Contagious Leadership*. It doesn't take scripted words; it doesn't take mission planning; it doesn't take anything other than the mood you put in the air. Hersey says, "True leadership has more to do with who we are than what we do. Leadership occurs out on the skinny part of the branches, out where it is exhilarating and terrifying at the same time. The trouble is most of us have been hugging the trunk of the tree for so long we do not dare step out where the real rewards are found. The best way for a company to stand out is to dare to actually be that which every other company only dreams of being—a contagious leadership factory."

33. Be Ruthless with Your Loved Ones

Declare today "sacred time"—off-limits to everyone, unless
invited by you. Take care of your personal wants and needs.
Say no, graciously but firmly, to others' demands.

Oprah Winfrey

Don't let your family and loved ones abuse their access
to you during working hours. It does not serve them to
think you are at their command, like a baby commands a
bottle. It weakens them and makes them spoiled and
dependent.

It also makes you a nervous wreck. It takes your head
out of the game. For so many reasons—almost too many to
name—a constant influx of calls from your family runs
counter to the creation of wealth.

Of course you want them to have access. Of course if
there is a problem you want them to always feel free to call
you. But we have a friend named Ramon who had let this
get out of hand.

We were coaching his small office team, and he was
constantly getting calls. His wife called during one of our
coaching sessions to ask Ramon how to spell a word! He

was getting interrupted all day with such a frivolous family upset that it got in the way of the flow of wealth into his work.

Nothing speeds your success faster than *uninterrupted* time. Yet many people, like Ramon, no longer even know what that is.

If you have this problem, stop letting your family interrupt you all day. Because you don't permit your employees to interact with their families that way, do you? A full day of personal calls? When employees see you dealing with family affairs at the business, work life gets creepy for them. It gets creepy for your employees to know that your wife is on the line with a question about the dog's diet. That's off-putting for them. It changes the theme of the work mission for your employees.

You can cure all this by letting your family know that unless it's some kind of emergency, you would like to channel your talking with them into your lunch break, for example, and always out of earshot of your work partners.

We can't tell you how many business owners allow their spouses free reign. Every other hour, here the owner's spouse is calling! And he takes the call in front of everybody and starts saying things like, "No I think the green candles will be fine for tonight" and "Your mother? I don't care what your mother says!" And it just goes on and on and the employees feel so uncomfortable around this that it disconnects them from work altogether.

Remember that it will always be uncomfortable to your work partners to be exposed to the inner life and the travails of your marriage or family. And your spouse only does it because you've given her the message that it's okay.

It's important to be ruthless and kind simultaneously. You'll only have to do it once or twice. Explain to friends and family that you will succeed faster at work with full focus on work. Every time they interrupt that focus, your wealth is diminished. Do they really want that?

And you can also say, "When I talk to you, I want to be able to talk to you. I don't want to be distracted by business. I want to be able to focus on what you have to say. At work I can only half-listen to you, and I'm not going to do that."

You can get the family to see that it actually honors them to have a special time when you talk to them as opposed to giving them 24/7 round-the clock access just because you don't know how to say "no."

Remember, too, that the reverse of this is also true. When you're home with family, it's good to *be* with them.

Sam says, "I do a lot of work at my home, and they know that when I close the door, I'm focused on the work. Now if I want to stop working and do something with the kids—play with them— I stop work. I think multi-tasking is the worst thing I can do. A lot of people think, 'Oh, I can do two things at once' and then you do a bad job at both of them! I made a determination a while ago that if I was going to be with my kids, I didn't want to be working on work."

Because kids don't understand. They'll never understand why business has to be taken care of in their presence. They just think you've got something you would rather pay attention to than them. (Which is actually true in that moment.)

We were coaching a business owner named Aden who said, "My business takes up all my time right now—I don't have time for my family." And that was because Aden's business wasn't producing enough while he was at his business. So we gave Aden an assignment to take one day off a week, which was totally counter-intuitive for Aden, whose workplace was like a scene from WKRP with drama and chaos swirling all around.

But he rose to the occasion. Aden found out how he could get five days of work done in four days! He realized that when he was taking personal calls and getting involved in all kinds of fiascos at his business throughout those five days, they were ineffective.

Aden was shocked to find out "If work is just work, I can get everything I was doing done in four days."

We like to use the "Day Before Vacation" as an exercise for people who don't think they can do this. What they realize when they look back on the day they had right before going on vacation is that that day was an airtight, seamless day of no-nonsense efficiency! Knocking out task after task with no small talk or distractions. The day before vacation they were able to do about three days' work in one day! They were making sure everything got handled and completed prior to going on vacation because they weren't going to be there for a week. If anyone wanted to interrupt them with some non-work talk or office gossip, they would just say, "It's going to have to wait because I'm going on vacation tomorrow and I really need to get all this stuff handled because I'm leaving on a plane to Mazatlan in the morning and there's no way I can do it after that, so we're going to have to talk when I get back." And people would smile and say "great" and then leave. People get real ruthless with their time when they know they're about to go on vacation.

So it really can be done, and it can be done as an everyday practice!

Personal life and business life don't mix well. It will almost always affect your wealth creation in a profoundly negative way. That's why most larger companies have policies about not having immediate family members working together. The reason they have those policies is because they have learned the hard way. They have learned that family members become inappropriately emotional with each other. Long-standing family resentments infect the workplace like the flu. Family members do not behave as loyal employees seeking a common financial goal. They behave like family members working on their family issues and using the job as a pretense to do their unfinished therapy. Jealousies and envy are the daily themes.

Of course there are family businesses who end up thriving, but these people use tremendous discipline, and they are the exceptions.

If you've got family members who are only there because you think you've done them a favor by giving them a job and they couldn't get a job elsewhere, it really hasn't done them any favors. And in the end, a year later or 10 years later, you realize it's time for them to go. They would have been better off to have those two years back, out in the world, becoming independent, seeking their own way rather than just avoiding getting a real job because they knew you and they could work for you.

So in the end the more "ruthless" you are with your family, the faster wealth accrues to you and them! And the happier everyone will be.

34. Seek Rejection and Objection

All great innovation is based on rejection.

Louis Ferdinand Celine

When a customer says "no" to your offer, that's a valuable moment. It's not bad news because now you get to find out why.

If you really want to understand your customers' true needs and wants, this "no" moment is a wonderful moment. Because true and reliable information is about to come your way. Prior to this it might have been nothing but the dance of posturing.

Most people use rejection as an excuse to nurture hurt feelings. But wealth creation is a logical process. Leave the negative emotions out of it, and you'll soar. Put them in there all day long, and you'll tumble.

When a good employee quits, is that nothing but bad news? A reason to leave work early and go to a biker bar or the bakery? Not if you are tuned to the movements of true wealth-creation. If you're tuned in you'll want to have a really wonderful exit interview with that employee so you can find out all kinds of things about how to make your place a better place to work in. Much great innovation is based on rejection!

When somebody decides to turn down an entrepreneurial project that you have offered them, you want to light up, not shut down. Because you can now learn more from why you have been rejected than you ever could from having been accepted.

In years past, one of Steve's clients was Dick Tomey, the head football coach at the University of Arizona. Steve used to make recruiting videos for Tomey's team. While working with Tomey he noticed something unusual about him. Coach Tomey somehow seemed happier after a loss than he was after a victory.

"I asked him about that one day," Steve recalls. "I said 'Coach, you seem a little more on your game, upbeat, ready to go next week after you lose than after a victory. After a victory there's something a little worrisome about your mood.'

"And he said, 'I'll tell you why that is. When we lose a game, I can't wait to get to the films because we're going to learn a lot about ourselves. There are so many things we can do in practice next week to make us a better football team. When we win a game, we really don't have as many guidelines as to what to do and what to work on. We begin to feel a little invulnerable. So there's not as much to learn from it. My function as a coach isn't as easy and exciting for me after a win. Even though I much prefer to win (don't get me wrong and don't misread those expressions), I do feel after a loss that now my work is clear. Now me and the coaching staff really know what to do and now we've got an opportunity to build this team in the right direction given what our defeat revealed.'"

Coach Tomey's fantastic attitude can apply to all phases of professional life as well. Defeats are our greatest instructors. Whereas victories can put us to sleep.

The best thing you can have in any sale you are making, in any product you are making, any invention, any idea, is to get a "no" as soon in the process as possible. Most people can't see that. Most people spend their lives trying to isolate themselves from rejection. They think it's painful.

Try reversing that attitude. Go ahead and seek rejection. Seek objection. Go for it. Love it. Embrace it and study it. It will show you the way to create wealth for yourself faster than any success will. It will teach you so much! Because any time somebody tells you why your idea *can't* work, that's just showing you the flip side of how it *could* work! Just turn the coin over!

Thomas Edison failed in his attempts to invent the light bulb thousands of times. And people cite that example as an example of persistence. Dogged, mule-headed persistence. But it wasn't that at all. Edison didn't have to keep plowing through failure after failure, because they weren't failures to him. They were informative events! Wonderful feedback from the world! And that's all that rejection is. It's simple, informative feedback. We are free to interpret it as a negative, tragic rejection if we want, but that's optional.

35. Become Unreasonable
Once a Day

A life spent making mistakes is not only more honorable
but more useful
than a life spent doing nothing.

George Bernard Shaw

This one is a great drill for our coaching clients who are interested in creating more wealth no matter what their profession: Every day make at least one unreasonable request.

Ask for something big.

Steve remembers, "One day, many years ago, early in my career as a writer, I was wishing that I had 200 copies of one of my books because I had an idea for a promotion. But I couldn't afford them at the time, even at the author's rate. So I was just sitting around wringing my hands, wishing I had 200 books because of the opportunity I had with them. And at that time, fortunately for me, I was doing my stretch activity of making one unreasonable request a day. So I called the publisher and I made a request. I said, 'I request that you send me, without charge, 200 books. I've got something I want to do with them that's going to help the book in the long run.' And much to my surprise my publisher said, 'Okay. We'll send them right out. No problem.' A week later, five large boxes arrived with a total of 200 books in them, and they were sitting on my front porch! Just because I asked for them."

Sometimes, you can call someone and request their help, and they'll jump in and help you. In your own mind it might have been an unreasonable thing to do before you did it. But later both of you were glad you did.

The great playwright George Bernard Shaw became a very wealthy man in his day writing powerful, popular plays. He always said that our first duty in life is not to be poor. He also said, "The reasonable man adapts himself to the conditions that surround him... The unreasonable man adapts surrounding conditions to himself... therefore all progress depends on the unreasonable man."

If you're late with a payment, call someone, make the unreasonable request that we skip a couple of months and then we pick it up. And always remember to be okay with people declining any unreasonable request, because by its nature it's unreasonable.

But the more of those you learn how to do, the easier it is to do, and the more fun it becomes.

Recently, Sam asked a director of a TV station in Canada who was interviewing him if he could have his own TV show there. "Not now," he said. But still, it was fun that he asked, because you never know; they might have been searching that very day for something and might have said, "Why don't you come talk to us?"

So the key here is to ask for what you want in life. You'll be amazed at how many surprises are in store for you. Especially if you don't attach any meaning or significance to people declining the request.

A couple of years ago, Sam had to go into the office of someone who he was selling a piece of property to. There had been a comedy of errors that led to a contractual mix-up, and the bottom line was that Sam had to obtain

$353,000 that day or the deal wouldn't be possible. It would no longer be Sam's property to offer.

"It was funny," Sam said. "This guy owned a chain of fitness clubs, and he said he needed another two weeks to get the money. And I said I had to have the money that day. He was extremely busy with things, but I just sat there in his office. He asked me what I was doing and I said, 'The only way I can leave this office is if I have the money.' And he said, 'You know, you've got a lot of guts. You're just going to sit here until I give you $353,000?' And I said, 'You've got it.'"

Later that day Sam left with a check in his hand for $353,000.

People are shy and intimidated and afraid of other people. So they hold back. They don't ask for what they want. And then they get to the end of their lives and realize lying on their death beds that they could have asked for anything. Anything.

36. Get Some Help

We work on ourselves in order to help others,
but also we help others in order to work on ourselves.

Pema Chodron

There is a paradox in asking for help. It appears to be a sign of weakness and surrender, when, in truth, it is a sign of strength.

Not asking for help only means you have a bigger commitment to your story than you do to your wealth. Your story says you don't need help. That you are a rugged individual. Your story says you can do this on your own. A lone, solitary admirable figure standing tall among the weaklings. The story says you have something to prove to the world and darn it, you're going to.

But what if you were committed instead to success? What if you had *no interest* in building a heroic story and your sole focus was on creating vast amounts of wealth?

Then you'd get help.

For the same reason that Peyton Manning has a quarterback coach, Jim Carrey has an acting coach, and Celine Dion has a voice coach.

When you're more committed to success than you are to looking good, you will find someone to coach you.

Steve was confused and conflicted 17 years ago as his career as a marketing and advertising man was no longer going anywhere.

"I was at a crossroads and my professional life had no focus," Steve recalls. "I had pretty much ruled out any chance of succeeding financially in a big way. Then I met my coach."

That coach was the legendary Steve Hardison, who suggested that Steve Chandler attend a seminar with him about purpose, communication, and commitment.

"We were in there together for three days, and I created my entire future," Steve recalls. "When I got out I proudly announced my five-year plan to Hardison, and he just laughed.

Hardison said, "Five *years*?"

"What's wrong with that? It takes time to become well known as a speaker. It takes a lot of time for your name to get out there."

"Not in my world," Hardison said. "If I'm going to coach you, we're going to do this *right now*. I'm not real interested in the future."

Within a year *100 Ways to Motivate Yourself* was on its way to becoming an international bestseller, and Steve Chandler had become one of the most sought-after keynote speakers in the nation.

At first Steve didn't think he was ready to take his speaking and writing to the world.

"I don't have enough success yet to be credible," he told Hardison.

Hardison said, "Talk about your failures. Tell the truth. You'll be the only person out there doing that. Everyone else is trying to look good."

"What do I have to lose?"

"Nothing! You're not even alive right now compared to who you could be . . . who you really are."

So the months and years went by, and Hardison delivered his powerful, transformative coaching. Every time

Steve thought he'd reached his limit financially, his coach took him to a higher level.

"This is why I'm such a believer in coaching," Steve says. "This is why I wanted to be a coach myself. I've been a living example of what coaching can do."

Today the world is full of coaches. There are so many wonderful coaches practicing right now that no one should ever fail at anything.

Sam has received his own coaching from some of the best, including Dan Kennedy, who is world famous for transforming businesses from break-even to huge profits.

If you are looking for a coach, ask around. Ask people you know who are being coached. Most coaches will talk to you long enough at the start for you to get a good impression of their skills. We can also recommend coaches for you to interview, as well, as we now work with a large number of them. Contact us at www.stevechandler.com and we'll find you a coach.

Coaches see things you don't see. They come into your business and see immediate opportunities for greater profit. They also see things in *you* that you don't see. Most people we coach are living at about ten percent of their potential. They are weighed down like a pack mule with negative stories about themselves, the people around them, and the world itself. As these stories are lifted—which is what good coaching does—they find new freedom and courage to act.

Most people take very little action in any given day to create wealth. They truly don't. Most of the actions they do take are survival moves, designed to defend against misfortune.

Coaching takes you out of that defensive posture and allows you to open up to the infinite wealth of the universe.

37. Turn "Good" Business Away

Don't be too busy earning a living to make any money.

Joe Karbo

Make sure that you're turning customers away who can't pay your price. Or can't behave. Don't just negotiate with every single one of them out of need.

When you sell yourself at a lower level than you really want to, that now becomes *who you are* to the world. Word goes out that your work is great and your price is low. As a result, you attract more and more people looking for that great low price. You create exactly what you don't want. And you're so needy you can't stop it.

If you had been able to simply turn that business away, you would create more wealth in your life. It just didn't feel like you would. But we know the role of feelings in wealth creation. Toxic! Why not say to customers trying to jockey for a better price, "I'm sorry we can't work together right now. Maybe sometime in the future it will be a good match."

Start to establish in the mind of the world what your price is. That will serve you in the long run, because either the people you turned away will now come back with enough money to use you, or they'll put the word out that that's what you cost, and there will be a lot of people who gravitate toward you *because* of what you cost. Funny as that sounds. Because people always associate price with value.

Steve was once pursuing a really big business coaching contract for which he was turned down at the last minute. It turned out he was turned down because his fee was too low! And the company owner that was going to hire him said to a mutual friend, "Anyone whose fee is down at that level just absolutely cannot be as good as we thought he was. There's something wrong with him that we don't know about."

Steve recalls, "Yes, there was something wrong with me all right. I thought I was in need! I had gone into his office thinking I needed him more than he needed me. That's what was wrong with me."

How many times does that happen that we don't even know about? So turning business away is actually a good thing; it's not irresponsible.

Most people have an inner philosophy that says, "Never Say No to Money." Money is so scarce, money is so precious, that if you have any opportunity for it to come in your door in any way, you must say yes. It's the only responsible thing to do. So they think.

A lot of business people and sales people have the belief that they're like the government or like a charity, where they have to accept every single customer, just because they're a customer. The truth is, you don't need *every* customer; you just need *good* ones. And by good ones we mean, first of all, the profitable ones.

"We'll make it up in volume" is dysfunctional. "We'll never be undersold!" is equally dysfunctional. Because what if you're undersold by a company that's going bankrupt? Yes, you can and should let yourself be undersold.

"I hope everyone undersells me," Sam says, "because I want to provide the best value and be the most expensive. When I coach clients about raising fees, they get worried that if they raise their fees, they're going to lose customers and lose that business. But it never turns out badly. The few they may lose were their biggest headaches anyway, and they always end up gaining business because of their commitment to be worth more."

When Sam says he's always providing "the best value," he means it. A lot of business consultants sell their teleseminars at a nice price, as Sam does, but if a member of the group misses the call, too bad. Sam makes certain each conference coaching call is recorded and made into a CD and mailed to each member so that those who miss the call can play it. And those who were on the call "live" have a permanent version for playing as many times as they like. It's one of many values he *adds*. And he's always looking for more.

His love of being the "most expensive" is always matched by his love of giving the most value for the money. You can do the same.

38. Seize the Present Moment

In the middle of every difficulty lies opportunity.

Albert Einstein

Stories and movies that fueled our fantasies as children made wishing and hoping seem like positive exercises. Jiminy Cricket sang to the wishful side of all of us. But now that we are living adult lives, anything that catapults the mind into the wishful future creates stress and fatigue. It delivers that overwhelmed feeling that keeps us from that one fresh, clean action that would solve everything.

Because once we are in action, the world changes. The past and future drop away. Oxygen flows to the brain. Light enters where there was darkness. It is fun to be alive.

Noted psychotherapist Dr. Brad Blanton has discovered that "Wishing is a way to remove oneself from what is going on now. Hope is how most of us avoid growing up."

Back in the early 90s Sam was broke and sitting on his couch in Canada watching TV.

And a story came on TV about a two-dollar coin that just came out. They were having a problem throughout Canada because the cash register drawers were made to accept two-dollar paper bills but not coins. Cashiers were going to have a tough time pulling those coins out because they'd get stuck in the corners.

Sam was watching this feature story on TV, and he was totally broke at the time. And then the announcer on TV said, "We found one person that decided to make the new coin problem easier for everyone," and it was a young man that invented a little adapter that could fit into any cash register that would convert it from a bill drawer to a little coin drawer. It was just a little plastic insert, but it worked like a charm! And the first thing Sam thought was, "Oh man, why didn't I think of that?" Like everyone does when they see something like that on TV. But then the TV said that there were *thousands* of cash registers with this problem that have to be fixed.

So Sam did some searching around—this was in the days before the internet—and he called the TV station and said, "Hey I just saw that story. Can you give me some contact information for that person?" And he got the contact information and found out how he could buy a large number of the cash register insert devices wholesale.

But Sam was broke at the time. He couldn't even figure out how to pay his credit card bill. Therefore he had to get inventive about finding a way to buy a few cases of the coin-accepting plastic devices wholesale. But once he did that he went out to different malls and retail stores and started selling the inserts to them. Soon he was making $500 and $600 a day by switching over people's cash registers.

There were probably hundreds of thousands of other people who were watching TV at the same time who needed some money, too, but it never occurred to them to take any action. They may have even gone into further debt to order a video about dream visualization so that they could stay right there on the couch and picture things coming true. Most people watch TV in that dreamy state, envious of all they see, wishing life was different.

They haven't let themselves enter the present moment, much less seize it. They don't realize that opportunity is everywhere. There are always opportunities out there trying to present themselves to us, and until our minds enter the present moment, we just can't see them. The mind that is only wishing things were different is shut down to the opportunities that are right here right now.

Two thoughts round this out. One from Nathaniel Branden, the world's top psychologist of self-esteem, who says, "A goal without an action plan is a daydream." And then the simplest directions ever given for success from St. Francis of Assisi who said: "Start by doing what's necessary; then do what's possible; and suddenly you are doing the impossible."

39. Make Your Meetings More Meaningless

Don't judge each day by the harvest you reap
but by the seeds that you plant.

Robert Louis Stevenson

Everyone says meetings are boring. People automatically think their teams shouldn't have so many meetings.

But the real problem is that people don't have *enough* meetings. People don't communicate *enough*. They wait so long to meet that their meetings drone on with all the backed-up sludge that has been saved up forever, and attendees go to sleep.

Have your meetings be fresh and lively. Hold meetings often enough so that there is virtually no agenda that you have to follow. The more good, fun meetings you have, the better your group gets because you've increased communication and motivation. Everybody starts to understand each other better. It feels more like a team. People don't break off and Balkanize into little groups of "our department against yours."

Companies that are on the rise hold lots of meetings; the meetings are short, they're fun, and they promote understanding between people. People meet, and then they jump right back into the business.

We know and coach teams who meet every single day, early in the morning when they all gather together. They have kind of a rally. They sometimes even meet late in the afternoon for a review—how did we do, how can tomorrow be better? And those are the teams that are thriving.

If you want your meetings to be really exciting and good and fun, get different people to lead meetings; grow leaders in your company. You don't always have to have the same person leading the meetings. You want to spread leadership around the company and give everyone an opportunity to be in charge.

Think about meetings the same way that football teams think about huddles—here's what we're going to do: we're going to move forward in this direction.

Most companies run a no-huddle offense constantly. No one gets to talk or chime in with great ideas and observations. They're just winging it for weeks at a time, and then later they all suffer a long, boring meeting. Football teams huddle before every play, and there's a reason for that.

Another kind of meeting you want to have more often is what we call the "big picture" meeting, wherein everyone learns the point of everything. What's the meaning of life on these premises? Where we are heading? The grand vision. How everything fits together. Most companies wait for an annual retreat to do this, but it's too important a motivator to wait so long to do it.

And if you're doing business with partners, you'll want to meet often on the central issue of wealth creation. Most people never meet on that subject. They meet about problems. Soon they become a group of problem-solvers, instead of a group of wealth-creators.

Have this be the subject of a meeting: How does this adventure of ours expand, succeed, and get more creative?

And if you are in business alone, as so many people are today, don't forget your meetings! Meet with yourself for the very same objectives that a team would meet for. Let your conscious mind and your subconscious mind get to know each other. Let the left side of the brain shake hands with the right. Harmonious convergence leads to wealth.

40. Go Into Hiding

In solitude, where we are least alone.

Lord Byron

The great psychologist Rollo May once said, "It is an ironic habit of human beings to run faster when we have lost our way."

In today's information-overloaded world we have endless opportunities for input. It's easy for humans to create a whole life of reacting to input coming in from outside sources. We are bombarded.

But what about our output? Will it just be a reaction to that input, or will it be truly inventive? The great business guru Tom Peters likes to urge his audiences to hold out for inventiveness that is "insanely great!" That can't happen from a day of fending off input.

Most people just fend off that information like a hockey goalie fends off shots all day. So it's important to deliberately create a structure for countering that. A time to take the pads and face mask off and go think.

Yuri was a personal trainer who said to us, "I get my best ideas in the sauna. I don't know why this is. And sometimes I get my best business ideas while I'm on vacation! Why don't I get those ideas during the work day?"

Yuri didn't yet see that the reason that phenomenon happens is that the sauna and vacation are the only times he gives himself to really be alone and allow ideas to float up to the surface. If he were willing to have the courage to be alone more often, he'd get even more great ideas.

Therefore, it was important to teach Yuri how to counter his over-communicated life with deliberate pockets of silence, creativity, and isolation. To encourage him to go into hiding. Once he got the hang of it, he was delighted. You will be too.

Your best ideas come to you in silence, so it's crucial to learn to sit alone and have creative thinking time. No computer and no TV, because those are distractions from creative thinking. They can be destructive to your journey to wealth. They have their place, but so does silence.

People need to make room for that "Aha!" to happen. To create any wealth at any level. If you're a teenager looking for work, you can use the silence, too. Just take a long walk, just you and the birds and the breeze, and ideas will come.

One of the greatest sources of wealth is your own subconscious mind. But it needs time and space to express itself. It holds everything you need for wealth creation, and it's ready to help you. But if you have nothing but input coming into your mind all day, it can't help you. There's too much noise, and we live in an increasingly noisy world.

It used to be that you could relax in an airport before a flight and gather your thoughts. But now there's nowhere to sit without the cacophony of cell phone calls and CNN pounding your eardrums. It's an increasingly noisy world, and so silence becomes even more rare and valuable. Use it and you'll have a secret advantage others don't have. You'll be using the half of the biological computer that others simply do not use.

If you already have a little business of your own, silence is even more important for you, because the temptation is huge to seize the day every day by encountering all those people and situations that seem to be crying out for your attention. Make sure you balance that with sanity. Go away, sit on a park bench for an afternoon like a lazy person. Let solutions occur to you. Write them down. Don't bring your cell phone; leave it in the car. The most healthy thing you can do for wealth creation is to be alone, worry about nothing, meditate, take notes, and be away from distraction.

We coach small business owners to design ways to actually spend less time at the business, and their businesses always benefit from that.

A lot of times, business owners will say to us, "How can I get more things done?"

And we say, "Do you have an office at your business?"

"Yeah."

"Don't go into your office!"

"Where in the world do I go?"

"There's a secret place of productivity; it's called the library. You're not allowed to use a cell phone, and no one can talk to you. And it's the most underused business tool today. The library is perfect. They have those little cubicles, it's quiet, there are a whole bunch of resources you can go there and read, and you can get a lot of ideas just wandering down the different aisles of the library looking at random topics. Let your mind roam free. It's amazing."

The best strategy Sam ever had for increasing his creative money-making ideas involved his dog, Buster, who unfortunately died a few years ago. Sam called Buster "The Million Dollar Dog" and he would walk him three times a day!

"I would get terrific ideas just being able to walk with Buster. I was getting coaching at the time, and in one exercise I had to write down how I used my time during the day. And so I wrote 'three long dog walks' down, one in the morning and one in the middle of the afternoon, and again in the evening, and it looked on paper like a huge waste of time. But that was actually the most productive thing I did all day! Walking the dog!"

Microsoft's multi-billionaire Bill Gates takes a whole month off every year "just to think." Has that been effective? Forty billion dollars of personal wealth would suggest that it has. It's a habit worth paying attention to. A month off to do nothing. Because out of nothing comes something. Bill Gates' creativity moves forward more in that month "off" than in any other.

Your time alone will do the same for you. Forty billion? Don't rule it out.

41. Keep Thinking Bigger

The world we have created is a product of our thinking;
it cannot be changed without changing our thinking.

Albert Einstein

Steve recalls his early days as a public speaker. He wasn't sure anyone wanted to hear him speak at all, much less pay for it.

So he'd give free talks at Rotary Clubs, business breakfasts, professional women's groups, faculty gatherings, anywhere. And finally people would come up to him after his speech and say, "I enjoyed your talk today, I'd like to bring you in to talk to my company. What would you charge to give this talk in my company?"

And Steve would say, "$300," and they'd say, "Great!"

And pretty soon he was saying "$900," and they were saying, "Great!" And it wasn't long before he'd say "$2,000," and they'd say, "Wonderful."

Steve recalls, "It wasn't that I was getting that much better. It was really *me being able to say it* more than it was whether I was *worth it*," Steve remembers. "I had all those dark thoughts like, 'Am I worth it?' Then I found that you just have to be able to say it. And they can decide whether to pay it or not. And once they decide to pay it, you then make yourself worth it."

Two and a half years after his first series of free talks, his training company was receiving $40,000 a day for Steve to speak to leaders at a Fortune 500 high tech company.

Believe it or not, Donald Trump did not start his real estate empire with a lot of money. But he always had one thing going for him that the people around him did not have: a huge capacity for thinking big. Now he lectures young people at business schools and he always says, "As long as you're going to think anyway, think big."

42. Break the Binds of Linear Time

We only have this moment, sparkling like a star
in our hand....and melting like a snowflake. Let
us use it before it is too late.

Marie Beynon

We coach individuals. And we also coach businesses. And whenever we begin a coaching session and our clients report that things aren't going well, we notice that their minds are either in the future or they're in the past.

They're either wishing things were better and their head's in the future, or else they're thinking about things they wish they had done differently and they'd like a do-over. They may wish they hadn't hired that person, or they wish they hadn't bought that computer program.

For you to succeed it's really important that once you've got your game plan in place for the day, you learn to get out of the future. And once you've settled open-ended problems, you learn to get out of the past. Those two practices will allow you to bring everything you've got to the things you have decided to do right now.

It's okay to check in once in a while with your future to tune up your ideal scene and to look at your specific goal, but that's just to check in. Don't stay there! Because you'll start to get scared. (And this is because the future doesn't exist. It's frightening to live—as most people do—in a place that doesn't exist.)

Consulting your future plan is just to look down at the map one last time before you take the wheel again and start to fly. It isn't to live there. The map is not the territory. The menu is not the meal. Your plan exists as a brief reminder of what you're up to, so you can get right back into the moment and the opportunity at hand.

The more excellent you become at making the task at hand (that one thing that's in front of you at the moment) turn out beautifully, the faster you will succeed. All success occurs now. Not in the future. Not in the past. In the now.

The more excellent you are at talking to that one person you're talking to right *now*, the faster your wealth grows, because that person carries the experience of *you* out to the world. It's your *presence* that impresses people. Not your future.

Zen teachers say that true mastery is washing the floor when you're washing the floor, or lying in the hammock when you're lying in the hammock. You're not washing the floor thinking about how great it will be to lie in the hammock, and you're not lying in the hammock thinking, "Oh no, I've got to go wash the floor." You're just doing the thing that's in front of you. For ego-driven and needy westerners, this can take a lifetime at a monastery to learn. Or you can learn it now.

When you are preoccupied with the past, it leads to feelings of regret and resentment. Those feelings take you down to dysfunctional moods and states. You can't produce greatness while feeling that way.

When you're thinking all day about the future, you are filled up with worries, desperate wishes, and dark fears. What's standing right in front of you is neglected or poisoned by feeling scared. People walk away from you thinking, "Well, I'm not overly impressed with that person. I don't get a very confident feeling that they've got what I want."

The better you are in the present, the better your future will get. And the better you are in the present, the less emotional pull your past will have on you.

So once you've selected your activity (from your delicious menu of options!) jump into it, be focused on it, and bring tremendous creativity and excitement to it. Master the moment.

43. Pay Top Dollar

A second-class effort is a first-class mistake.

William Arthur Ward

Sam used to be obsessed with coupons. He would spend enormous amounts of time sorting through them looking for the tiniest advantage.

"I wanted to charge top dollar, but I wanted to pay rock bottom," he said. "Now I see it's better if it works both ways. I no longer mind paying a bigger price. As a matter of fact, when I'm negotiating with people, and I don't want to sound like a fool or something, but when I negotiate with business people I don't try to strip them down to the lowest possible price. I say, 'Listen, this has to work for both of us and I don't want you to quote me a price that's going to be something that you can't live with or you're not going to make a profit on. I don't expect you to work for free; I certainly don't.'"

To attract more wealth into your life, you want people you deal with to be well paid. If you're not looking to take advantage of people, in the future that fairness will come around to serve you.

Because if you have a customer that's not grinding you down to the lowest possible price, you appreciate that customer. You really value their business. In the future if you can do something extra for them, you do. If you have two deadlines to be met: one from a person who grinds you down to the last nickel, and the other from a person you're making a good profit on, who are you going to deliver to?

Therefore you don't want to grind people either. And, psychologically, paying top dollar frees you up. The flow of money has a lot to do with psychology. And once you begin paying more, it becomes easier to charge more. It's quite disconnected if you preach "charge a lot" but are unwilling to pay a lot.

Steve was recently asked to speak at a company event where the business owner's name was (we will say) Lester. The minute the negotiations began for the event, Lester started trying to reduce the speaking fee and extend the amount of speaking time. Steve began making adjustments to Lester's requests in good faith but began to sense something odd.

"It was the tone of his negotiations," Steve remembers. "Lester was edgy and suspicious, like I was trying to take him. When I talked to his vice president, the vice president said he did that with everybody. He fights everybody for every penny."

Lester was not atypical. There are many Lesters out there today so scared about money that they fight everyone who wants it. They think their manhood (survival) is being threatened every time they spend money. So they end up poisoning their relationships throughout the day with their anger and fear.

Steve never did speak for Lester at that company event. They brought in a speaker who gave Lester a massive discount and then delivered what Lester later said was "the most boring speech my people have ever had to sit through." Lester even tried to get his money back.

Steve later said that if Lester had gladly paid the original price, he would have gone the extra mile for Lester's company.

"After I had lunch with him there was a lot I saw I could do to help his sales efforts improve," Steve said. "I was looking forward to making a real difference. But after he melted down and got neurotic about the money, I knew we had to part ways."

People who are scared and nervous about their lack of money receive less money from the universe. The scriptural saying is, "To he that has it shall be given, to he that has not, even that shall be taken away."

Look at what was taken away from Lester. A chance to turn his struggling sales program around.

Sam enjoys running his business success seminars well-dressed in the finest suits. He also enjoys pulling up to the building in a beautiful sports car. And it's not ego. It's an expression to his clients of prosperity. It's a visual symbol of the very place Sam takes them!

"If they're paying me top dollar and people see me pull up in a nice car, or I've got some nice clothing on, or I've just flown in from south of France, they pay me top dollar more easily, because they just identify me with living at that upper level, and being that kind of person. There's something about going first class in life that has a nice affect on your clients. They are warmed by it. You're not trying to play some Discount Guy role. It gives your clients a nice feeling that they've got the best person available."

And people don't want to do business with someone who looks like they're going to be out of business tomorrow. You don't want to be taking advice from a person who looks like they're not making enough to take care of themselves. You don't want to feel that guilty. You want your money to get results. So you want to pay it to someone who embodies results. The symbol is important because it communicates.

Sam started his business small. He was renting space to teach music and dance lessons to children. After his businesses kept growing he began buying land and doing construction. He found that when it came to getting bids from firms to do the construction, there would be three quotes, and common wisdom said to always take the lowest bid. On the surface it makes sense. Why pay any more than you have to?

One contractor was desperate for Sam's business because he hadn't worked for a while and consequently low-balled the quote to get the business. He started planning the job for Sam, and three weeks later when they were scheduled to start the construction, the contractor got a call from his buddy who said, "Hey, I got this work on this new hotel that's coming in. The pay's great. You want to start?"

"Aw, I committed to this Sam Beckford job already, but to tell you the truth, I'm not making any money on this job. So I'm just going to drop it. Who cares? I'll be there to work with you on the hotel!"

So a whole month was lost due to the paying-bottom-dollar syndrome.

"I'm not afraid to pay top dollar now," says Sam. "Paying bottom dollar costs too much."

44. See Everything as Practice

Happiness is not a state to arrive at, but a manner of traveling.

Samuel Johnson

The greatest soccer player of all time, Pele, was asked when he found time to practice, with all the touring and promotions he was doing around the world. He smiled and he said, "Everything is practice."

And he later said that what he meant was this: The way he walks up to the plane, the way he treats the flight attendant, the way he deals with his anxiety during turbulence, the attention he brings to gathering his bags, the precision he brings to all activities, and the energy he brings to little things all constitute practice. Life offers us wonderful opportunities for practice. Yet most people think it's worthless down time.

But that's why Pele became world famous and they didn't.

So if you've got an upset customer, if you've got a problem with a partner, or if you've got anything going on that you wish wasn't going on, you can reframe it in your own mind and see it as practice.

If you have a problem at home, if you have difficulty with a relative many miles away who's calling asking you to help them with some unsolvable personal problem, it really is practice.

If you drop the cup you are carrying and it breaks into a mess on the floor, it's another odd but useful form of practice. If you are stuck in a traffic jam, again, it's practice.

Because you can have *everything* you do tune you to a truer vibration.

There isn't anything that can't be practice for what you are going to do to create wealth.

Sam says, "Any time I'm in a bank line, I'll think, this is an exercise in patience. Am I just going to let it freak me out and get all mad and get up to the counter and lose it and complain that there should be more tellers on and this is unacceptable? Or is it going to be something that's going to increase my inner practice of quiet resolve, and teach me to find peace internally, and not in external circumstances."

Trivial upsets are a beautiful opportunity to study the relationship between thinking and being upset.

Most people have the long bank line be the *cause* of the upset. But practice allows us to eventually master the observation that it's only our thoughts that upset us.

Practice allows us to try thinking, "What a wonderful place to just chill and not be frantic, and I'll just stand here peacefully and let my batteries recharge and not have to be anywhere and not have to be upset like I used to be by a line like this."

You can use anything in your world to practice becoming more mindful and better-tuned to the true source of your emotional energy.

Here's what two masters of the art of practice, Michael Murphy and George Leonard, have to say in *The Life We Are Given,*

Practice your physical routine
Practice graceful communication
Practice planning
Practice meditation
Practice extraordinary service to others
Practice your professional magic

They also say, "When wisely pursued, practices bestow countless blessings. If we do not obsess about their results, they make us vehicles of grace and reveal unexpected treasures. In this, they often seem paradoxical. They require time, for example, but frequently make more time available to us: They can slow time down, and open us to the timeless moment from which we have arisen. They require sacrifice, but they restore us. While demanding the relinquishment of established patterns, they open us to new love, new awareness, new energy; what we lose is replaced by new joy, beauty, and strength. They require effort, but come to be effortless. Demanding commitment, they eventually proceed like second nature. They need a persistent will, but after a while flow unimpeded. Whereas they are typically hard to start, they eventually cannot be stopped."

Wealth flows to people who have inner strength and grace. It flows to those who have learned to master every moment of their day—not to those who have "bad days" and worry all the time. You can begin a total transformation of your life energy by seeing everything you do as practice.

45. Create Your Responses

Either you will make your life work, or your life will not work.

Nathaniel Branden

We get contacted by a lot of people whose lives are not working. They want coaching. They want their lives to work again.

But they don't see.

When we ask them to describe what they think is wrong, mostly what we hear about is other people. Other people disappoint them. Or tick them off. Or scare them. We know right away why their lives are not working: they are constantly trying to win the approval of others.

A life of expectation is a life of disappointment. A life of trying to win the approval of others is a life of fear and reaction. Wealth is a *creation*, not a reaction, and therefore it improves your capacity to earn when you learn to stop reacting to others.

It's never your life that's not working. It's always just you. But that's the best news there could ever be. Because you don't have to rearrange the world to make your life work. You just have to rearrange your approach.

When the Dalai Lama was asked if he wasn't angry at the Chinese for taking over his country Tibet, he replied, "Why should I give them my mind as well?"

Some people think the Dalai Lama's answer to that question was profound. They think he was able to answer that way because of his advanced spiritual practice.

But his is a response available to all of us. All we have to do is learn to respond rather than react. I can respond to other people, which has the elements of creativity and purpose in it, or I can react, which has the element of a teased animal in it. You tease a vicious animal and he will react. It's completely emotional.

Most people just react like that animal. They've descended into that low automatic defensive habit, and now it's just in their muscle memory to react. They get an email from the boss and they react. The chemicals are launched in the body, and an angry reply shoots out of the lips of the person so people in other cubicles can hear it. Some people save their most unconscious, knee-jerk reactions for when they get home. The spouse says something and they react. The child leaves a cookie on the carpet and they just react to that. (They were ready. They were waiting for something to react to.)

There is another way to live that's much wiser and happier. But it requires a mind shift. A shift up from the low gear of reacting. A shift up to the higher, smoother gear of responding.

You get a nasty email. You might feel like reacting with a cutting reply. You are justified. The email was absurdly unfair to you. But that's just a reaction. Any animal can (and does) do that. Do you just want to be a stimulus-response machine? You can become creative instead. Instead of reacting to the email, you will craft a response based on what you want that relationship to be. The big picture. Wouldn't your wealth curve be better served if your relationship with this person kept improving rather than going up and down riding the waves of testy reactions and come-backs?

Reaction: "This email is typically short-sighted and unmindful of the scope of the work I've put in."

Response: "Wow. I really got from your email how this is not a happy situation for you. Let's you and me talk it through. How about 4:15 in your office today? I look forward to talking with you."

As you learn to create responses to people rather than just reacting to them, you'll notice your life starting to work for you. You'll notice your success starting to flow inward because there is no longer any more resistance to others. They all become a part of the same evolution from fear to love. Love what you're doing and the money will follow.

46. Invent a Numbers Game

The acquisition of money is not a serious business;
it's a game that you play.

Stuart Wilde

Remember the long walks we took down the long trails as kids through the dreary beauty of the dying leaves on the trees and one of us shouted, "I'll race you to the barn!" And all of a sudden we were off! The tired legs and weary bones were no longer our reality. We had shifted reality with the words, "Race you to the barn!"

Can you really shift reality? Isn't reality defined as something you can not shift? Your mind, maybe, but not reality!

Reality has to come through your mind to get to you. So yes you can shift it. And numbers sure help, given that the universe is nothing but one glorious symphonic math equation.

Numbers that are painfully precise, down to the penny, like our rent, our mortgage, our light bill, our car repair bill, and our grocery tab are always other people's numbers.

And usually, they're the only numbers that we take seriously. They're precise numbers that drive our activities, but they're not ours! And unless we replace those numbers or have them be insignificant compared to our own numbers, we're always going to live a life of reaction and feel like we're living other people's dreams instead of our own.

If your quest for wealth is stuck, you can break out and increase your energy by getting a different kind of numbers game going.

If you're stuck, if you're frustrated, or if things aren't moving in a profitable way, don't just *try* to do it better. Put a number up on the wall!

If you're frustrated with recruiting, put a "3" on the wall. Now you're going to interview three people a week for the next ten weeks. Put a big star next to the three on your wall every time you hit it. You've got a game going.

If you've decided to generate a certain number of new clients by the midpoint of the year, put that precise odd number up everywhere.

These number-postings can work with obtainable process goals such as: how many calls a day you will make, or how many thank-you postcards you're going to send out, or how many new customers you'll personally talk to, or how much money you'll save per month, or how many visits to the health club you'll make per week.

Or they can be outcome goals, like the number that signifies increasing last month's income by 20 percent. Or that number of new clients. And the more numbers the merrier! Because the more numbers you create, the more numerical targets you put in your conscious mind. These numbers allow your subconscious mind to work for you. And it will do so even while you sleep. Notice how you can program your subconscious to wake you up at 5:55 in the morning. That's child's play to the subconscious mind. It can do bigger tricks than that in the daytime. It just wants the exact numbers.

With numbers, your life can take on a game element at work. Now you're responding to your own numbers rather than other people's numbers. It feels like a created life, because it is. It feels good.

Most of us are always responding to *other people's numbers*. We get bills from other people, so we look at the numbers on the bill and try to figure out when we're going to pay them. It's all coming in from the outside. The mortgage company wants a number, and the daycare wants a number. Everybody wants something and it's always got a number on it.

The way to turn this around is to have all the numbers you think about be your own. Because wealth is going to be a numbers game anyway, why not have it be directed by *your* numbers? Numbers that you have put up there on the wall that you want to hit.

When you wake up in the morning and see your own numbers, you feel like you're creating your own life—not just reacting to other people's demands. You'll no longer have a life of trying to hit other people's numbers.

When we meet with sales people to coach them, we ask them what it is they want to achieve. And if the sales person says, "Well, here's what the company wants me to do and here's where they've set the bar and here's what I need to do for them to pay me a bonus," we finally say, "Those are all *their* numbers. We're not interested in that. What do *you* want to do? What numbers do *you* want to hit? Let's get your life into that category."

And when we do that the sales person really picks up and gets excited. Soon she's laying out her own strategy for success with numbers that are bigger than the company's.

Sam says, "One of the things I've been doing for years, since I really started making substantial increases, was to have some numbers right beside my desk that I look at every single day. I revise them from time to time. They're ultimate business goals. I want to hit this; I want to hit that. And any time I'm stuck and I don't know what to do, I look at those numbers and I say, 'Okay, what's *one thing* I can do to get me closer to that goal right now?' And that's the one thing that can really be the magnet that pulls you back into the present moment. It doesn't have to be a list of every single goal you want to accomplish, but just a couple of key numbers at your fingertips."

One of the best things a salesperson can do is to stick those numbers on the visor in their car. When they flip the visor down, they're reminded of what the whole thing's about. It's not about going in and spending two hours with the customer chatting about the golf game they had this weekend. It's about the number on the visor.

Your numbers re-orient you to what you're up to. They serve you like territory coordinates serve a pilot or a missile launcher. Start putting them up around your house and office and feel the energy you get from them.

Remember, it's not what the number *is* that's important. It's what the number *does*.

47. Start All Over Every Day

All appears to change when we change.

Henri-Frédéric Amiel

Never stop reinventing yourself and reinventing your profession. Don't let habitual patterns of thought keep you stuck at any stage in your growth. Start every day with a fresh start. Don't get into a rut.

The only difference between a rut and a grave is a few feet.

If you run a small business or if you offer a professional service, or even if you're in an organization where you have a salaried job, ask yourself, "How can I do this work in a fresh and innovative way?"

Because that's exactly how people get ahead. They come up with new ideas and do things in an innovative way.

Don't just do things because that's how you did them yesterday. Be new to yourself every day. Refresh, reboot, and reinvent your work as often as you can. You can save what's good while trying all kinds of new things.

This approach of continuous reinvention will keep your mind fresh. You'll be amazed at how many new ideas you get from taking this approach of starting over every day.

Most people we coach have a secret life. In it, they think they will never change. They see themselves as permanent people. Fixed personalities. They don't see how to challenge that. Like the great Leonard Cohen song *In My Secret Life* says, "I saw you this morning/ You were moving so fast/ Can't seem to loosen /my grip on the past/ I smile when I'm angry/ I cheat and I lie/ I do what I have to /do to get by/ But I know what is wrong/ And I know what is right/ And I'd die for the truth/ In My Secret Life."

The truth is this: the mind-shift out of that imprisoned secret life can be easy. You have a mind, but you are not your mind. So you can shift it, just like the gear box in a car. The hard part is shifting when you don't think you want to.

Many doctors say they keep recommending to their patients who suffer from depression that they start to get up and exercise. Even a little. Just walk around a little bit. But the patients are too depressed to do it. They don't "feel like" walking, they say, even though their doctors are certain that moving the body would begin to lift the depression!

But somewhere, somehow, someone must do what he doesn't feel like doing for a true mind shift to happen. It's got to start somewhere. Someone has to do something they know they don't "have to" do.

And the minute you do that, you have a fresh start. You're no longer who you used to be.

48. Know Your Customer Better

If you work just for money, you'll never make it, but if you love
what you're doing and you always put the customer first,
success will be yours.

Ray Kroc

Most people struggling with wealth deprivation are
focused on themselves all the time. They focus on their
shortcomings and their worries. To reverse that struggle,
the trick is to get out of yourself completely.

Try focusing on someone else. Start with your
customer.

What can you do for your customer today that would
absolutely astonish and delight that customer? Even if you
don't have a literal external customer to interact with, everyone you work with and talk to can become your customer.

We all have people who are receiving the service of
whatever it is we do for a living. So we want to get out of
our own self-obsession and get into the minds of the people we are serving.

We can begin by asking, "What could I do that would
really help that person?"

Most people never ask that question. They're so focused on their own wants and needs that they don't see that there are people in life just waiting to be served. Those people are also waiting to reward that service.

If you get out of your own mind and enter other people's, you'll find out what they will pay you for and why. The better you understand customers, the more customers will trust you, pay you, and increase their activity with you.

If you're working at an organization where you don't deal directly with customers, you can concentrate your attention on everyone who can speak up for you and promote you down the line. So you'll get to know your manager better, your teammates better, and the people in the other departments better. Know what really serves them and how you can help.

Most people have so many layers of fear and suspicion of other people that they don't know them at all. But you can't really serve someone you don't know. So get out of yourself, get interested in others, study their wants and needs; it's one of the fastest roads to the elevated moods that lead to wealth.

Exactly why does your mood elevate? Because it's impossible to be depressed while you're truly helping someone else. The mind can't hold both things at once.

And what, again, is the connection between that elevated mood and wealth?

Wealth flows faster to happy people. Because happy people are in elevated moods. And those elevated moods are where the best ideas come from. And your highest energy! You can discover this immediately by trying an experiment. Get in front of your team and tell them they have a big problem and it must be solved. Then spend an hour discussing the problem and see what kind of solutions you get.

Then go in front of another team with the same problem, but a different approach. This time you are going to "brainstorm nutty possibilities" and have fun thinking out of the box. There is no problem, but there is a "subject" you'll center the brainstorm on. The brainstorm, when done right, is fun. Everyone participates, it goes round and round the room at a dizzying pace, and the funniest ideas are celebrated. But something strange also happens. Your people are so inspired by the elevated mood of the room that they come up with truly creative ideas. Real solutions!

This is not a theory. We do this with groups we coach all the time, and they are startled to see the results. By transforming the subject from "problem" to "interactive brainstorm," we create something magical. People aren't focused on themselves anymore. They're tuned into what the great psychologist Carl Jung called the "collective unconscious," that ultimate interconnected network of all minds at once.

49. Find Out Who You Really Are

What is it that you like doing? If you don't like it, get out of it, because you'll be lousy at it. You don't have to stay with a job for the rest of your life, because if you don't like it you'll never be successful in it.

Lee Iacocca

Continue your quest for self-discovery. Because the more you align your true talents with your work, the faster wealth is attracted to you.

A lot of people make fun of self-help, new age, self-discovery, and going on the inner journey. They ridicule it and say, "Hey, come on, that's woo-woo stuff. Get practical!"

But it's important to unpeel the protective layers you've built over the years. Find out who you really are. Discover how you want to serve people. Be conscious of your real loves, and what your real talents are—always know what you're really good at.

As you grow and evolve, you'll keep finding out more and more about yourself. If you keep that self-inquiry alive, it allows you to keep moving, very subtly, into areas where you can serve even better and be more appropriate to making money. You don't drop everything you've accomplished. You include it and transcend it simultaneously.

Because the more in alignment you are with what you were really meant to do for a living, the faster wealth will come to you. The old saying, "Do what you love and the money will follow" has proven to be true for us and for hundreds of our clients.

Doing "what you love" doesn't have to require an immediate drastic career change. You don't have to change overnight from one profession to another to have wealth begin to flow. It can be more subtle than that. You can start it right now inside whatever your current profession is. Keep moving to the part of the work you love, and keep loving the part you're working on.

Our client Rachel said, "I don't know what I love, I don't know what I want, and I don't know what I'm good at."

"Did you ever spend any time really looking into it?"

"No, I just seem to move from one crisis to the next. My life feels like it's always about what other people are asking me to do."

"Do you love always seeking their approval?"

"Approval? It's never enough, so no. I mean, even when I get it, I don't trust it. It doesn't last. It makes everything be about their feelings, not mine."

"Good observation. You're on the right path."

"But doesn't money come from service?"

"Yes, absolutely, but service is pure and free. It isn't an attempt to win someone over. It serves and moves on gracefully."

This was the perfect time for Rachel to get out of her story that told her she needed to win approval. This was a perfect time for self-discovery. She could now really look into her heart and find out what she was good at. Once she did that she was able to pick up her spirits and energy and direct them to greater success right away. She transferred to the part of the company she always wanted to work in and got an immediate promotion there. Self-discovery will do that. It has practical financial value. So don't wait too long to plunge in. (Pay attention to the old Sufi saying, "You have three days to live and two are gone.")

One of the few things Sam remembers from college was a course he took that studied a survey of people in their 80s. The survey had asked, "If you could do your 80 years over again, what would you do differently?" And the three most frequent answers the octogenarians gave were (1) Risk more, (2) Reflect more, and (3) Do more things that live on after me.

They received that enlightenment in their 80s! You might just want to adopt it now. What would life be like if you did? What would happen right now if you risked more, reflected more and did things that will live on after you?

50. Wash Your Brain Clean

The wise and moral man
Shines like a fire on a hilltop,
Making money like the bee,
Who does not hurt the flower.

The Pali Canon

Maybe some people had a little jolt of guilt buying this book! Like "Isn't this awfully selfish and greedy for me to want to learn ways to create wealth for myself?"

But when people get excited about the positive, helpful side of wealth, they can start a guilt-free prosperity project. It may be a home business working in the evenings and over the weekend, even while doing their day job. And if they put enough love and foresight into this little hobby business, it will rise up and overcome the day job and become the primary source of income for this lucky person. Fantasy? No, we work with many people who have done this very thing!

But the first step is always to clean the mechanism.

Many say that when someone is rich, they're *filthy* rich.

And when someone is poor, they are pristine and poor and saintly and clean.

And those are just thoughts, and your thoughts can slow you down. If you want to create wealth that flows freely to you like water from a well, you need to clean those wealth-related thoughts. And be able to think of being clean *and* rich, instead of being filthy rich.

Remember that most of the dirty thoughts attached to money have been put there by people who are envious. They're actually green with envy. Have you ever seen a sick person turning green? Envy is a sickness. It leads to unhealthy resentments and low levels of energy.

So for money to flow to you, money has to become clean energy in your thoughts. Cleaner than oil or nuclear energy. And it's got to be able to move things. Money can move a family from a poor part of town to a nice neighborhood. One clean move.

When we hold money to be clean and clear energy, it's much more fun to earn it and expand its presence in our lives. Metaphors move mountains. "Filthy rich" will make you feel dirty. Why not make a "clean sweep?"

51. Get Into Your Mind

Life is a comedy for those who think, and a tragedy
for those who feel.

Horace Walpole

When Napoleon Hill wrote *Think and Grow Rich*, his
whole point was about learning to direct your mind and
thought processes. If you really learned to think, you could
become wealthy.

His book is still popular today, for good reason. His
process works. His insights were revolutionary. People can
change their fortunes by changing their thinking no matter
how adverse the external conditions seem right now.

"Every adversity," said Hill, "every failure, every
heartache carries with it the seed of an equal or greater
benefit."

Napoleon Hill was born into poverty in a two-room
cabin in the town of Pound in rural Virginia. His mother
died when he was 10 years old. That heartache carried the
seed of a great benefit, however, when Hill's new step-
mother became the most inspiring person in his life.

She worked with him daily to build his confidence in
himself. She taught him to think. And because of her inspiration he began writing as a "mountain reporter" for small-

town newspapers at the age of 13! He used his earnings as a reporter to enter law school but soon had to withdraw for financial reasons. The turning point in his career was in 1908 with his assignment, as part of a series of articles about famous men, to interview industrialist Andrew Carnegie who at the time was one of the richest men in the world. Carnegie believed that his own success could be duplicated by anyone who used his simple formula.

Carnegie commissioned Hill to take that formula to the world. He provided Napoleon Hill with letters of reference to interview over 500 successful men and women, many of them millionaires, in order to prove that all of them were also using this simple formula, whether they knew it or not! Hill was given the job of publishing this formula for success. So he interviewed many of the most famous people of the time, including Thomas Edison, Alexander Graham Bell, Henry Ford, and Theodore Roosevelt. The project lasted over 20 years, during which time Hill became an advisor to Carnegie. The formula for success that Hill and Carnegie formulated was published initially in 1928 in his book *The Law of Success*. Later he compressed it into *Think and Grow Rich*.

Hill's (and Carnegie's) system for success was a process he called "autosuggestion," by which he meant the harnessing of the power of thought. Think about something enough and it can't help but come into your life. It will automatically suggest itself to you once it's found a neural pathway in your brain.

Hill said, "Your ability to use the principle of autosuggestion will depend, very largely, upon your capacity to concentrate upon a given desire until that desire becomes a burning obsession."

Although his books are somewhat dated in their language and social attitudes, the magic formula still applies, and we can learn a lot from him. And so many people forget his most shocking message: becoming rich is not about being a genius or having a high IQ. His formula can be used just as easily by *the average person* as it can by a genius.

Autosuggestion works because it is the opposite of taking all your suggestions from the outside world. Once you give up doing what everyone else suggests that you do, your life will take off. You will be ready to think and grow rich.

Becoming wealthy is a logical thinking process that can get messed up by emotional input. The logical road to wealth always gets you there when followed. We only get sidetracked when our negative anxieties pull us astray.

Fear is the most dangerous emotion on the way to wealth because it robs you of so much energy. Maintaining a fear requires enormous ongoing mental energy. It's like juggling. Ever try to juggle bowling pins? That's the job of the average worried mind. Fear is high-maintenance.

And even when that fearful energy gets converted to resentment and anger, it's still all that energy wasted! It's energy that could, instead, be used to create wealth. Plans for serving others could be created with all that energy being funneled into resentment.

We've heard employees at a small restaurant complain that they've had a bad day at work because for some reason they were "slammed" all afternoon.

"What do you mean by slammed?"

"People. Just slammed us. Wouldn't stop coming. We thought we'd catch a break in the afternoon, but we didn't."

Notice that these workers were actually working against wealth. There was a serious emotional disconnect between those employees and the owners of the restaurant. A disconnect that the owners are responsible for. A disconnect caused by the owners' fear of sharing the wealth (and therefore the mission) with their employees.

In larger companies, fear undermines wealth also. For example, most employees subconsciously work *against* getting promoted. They fear and resent their employers and therefore do not go the extra mile in their work and advance. Their energy goes to the fear instead of the work.

If they were able to take all negative emotion out of their work and just gently and joyfully work on, they would win advancement. But emotion creeps in and undermines wealth.

Every client we coach confronts the primary issue: Do you want your life's energy to go into fear or into wealth?

When Jonathan Swift said, "A wise man should have money in his head, not in his heart," he was onto something. Money is a mind game. We lose when we make it an emotional heart game.

As you create more wealth do not forget to honor yourself by cultivating your mind and releasing your emotions. A lot of us emerge from childhood and adolescence with really low self images. Perhaps well-meaning parents have told us, "You're never going to measure up; you don't even know how to clean up your room. You didn't give your schoolwork much of an effort; you're probably not going to make much of yourself." And so you come out of childhood, quite often, thinking, "Well, I better get some kind of minimal job that makes some basic minimal money, given how unsuited I am to measure up to big success." And that interior fear-based approach doesn't serve you. Everyone has something that they're really, really good at, and if they could just get it into alignment with the right profession and service of others, they would make a lot of money.

And "a lot of money" can mean different things to different people, which is good. Sometimes it starts small and just blossoms. We know a person right now who became a millionaire by taking care of other people's kids, then running preschools. And it didn't sound like a glamorous thing to begin with. Just watching other people's kids! But it was what she was great at and what she loved.

That's the power of the human mind at work.

52. Convert Your Dreams

A goal without an action plan is a daydream.

Nathaniel Branden

Put your dreams away after you've glanced at them at the start of the day. And by that we don't mean just give up. We mean don't get hypnotized by the dream.

A lot of people *only* dream. They never take a step to make the dream real. So do something to make that dream you had a reality. Don't just let it exist as a dream.

Southwest Airlines Herb Kelleher said, "We have a strategic plan. It's called doing things."

Most people we coach think their best dreams can't be acted upon yet. They are missing too many pieces. They might want to start a new career or new business, but they have to wait until they have the capital, or wait until they're in the right situation.

But there's never a perfect time for anything bold.

There's no perfect time to start a business, and no perfect time to take chances. There's a choice of potential bad times! So choose one of them and just go. Start converting that thing that's just a dream into reality, even if it's nothing other than the first step of registering the business name, registering a domain name, deciding to do something to actually bring it forward. Read a book about it! Open a file. Set a time each day to be with the dream for a half hour. Call it Execution Time. Take tiny steps to *execute* the dream.

Once your dream becomes a project rather than just a hoped-for thing in the future, you start to experience a quickening. Because energy flows to execution. It doesn't flow to daydreams. Daydreams are narcotic. Energy flows to action. Once you're in action, you're getting the wishing and hoping out of your system. Now you're out of the dream category and into the execution category. And the project lives differently in your mind. It's an active project! So when someone brings up something related to the dream, you can say, "I'm working on a *project* in that area right now; let's talk."

Instead of, "I've always dreamed of doing something like that."

Michael Korda in his book *Ulysses Grant* emphasizes that Grant was Lincoln's greatest general because he had a bias for action. He writes, "This adolescent incident of getting from point A to point B is notable not only because it underlines Grant's fearless horsemanship and his determination, but also it is the first known example of a very important peculiarity of his character: *Grant had an extreme, almost phobic dislike of turning back and retracing his steps.* If he set out for somewhere, he would *get* there somehow, whatever the difficulties that lay in his way. This idiosyncrasy would turn out to be one the factors that made him such a formidable general. Grant would always, always press on—turning back was not an option for him."

People come up to us and say, "Wow, I'd love to write a book. How do you write a book?" Guess what? We'll give you a little secret. You sit down and you get this secret device; it's called a pen. And you start writing it.

"A what? A pen? Where do I get one of those?"

People would rather dream.

Have your book or your website or your new profession be a project, not a dream. And then give it your attention. Sometimes the extra five minutes you give to your project after you've decided to quit on it kicks you into a strange new gear—a powerful new zone. This doesn't happen all the time, and when it doesn't, you've lost nothing. Just quit after those five minutes. *But*—it happens *enough* to really surprise you that you had so much more to give, and you had energy left you didn't know you had. You thought you were too tired to go on. But that was just a thought. You don't have to believe your thought. A thought is just a thought.

And this reminds us of William James when he said: "Most people never run far enough on their first wind to find out they've got a second. Give your dreams all you've got and you'll be amazed at the energy that comes out of you."

Taking action on a dream is something Sam learned in college. He was sitting in the cafeteria late at night. It was after 11 o'clock and he was studying. Suddenly someone came in and said, "Hey there's this group that sells books door-to-door, and you can win a prize to Mexico if you sell a certain number of books. Dino, the kid that won it this year, he can't go, and he's going to sell his ticket, which is airfare and accommodations for a week, and you get to go down with 30 other college students to Mexico. He's going to sell his ticket for $200!"

Sam looked out the window at the ice storm gathering in chilly Canada and said, "Wow, I'm going!" because Mexico was a long-standing dream of his.

And his friends sitting around him in the cafeteria said, "But you can't do that."

"Why not? I've got $200 in the bank. I can do that for sure."

"But you know it's leaving tomorrow; you can't just get up and go."

"Why not?"

"You just can't; you just can't do that."

They were all studying for the same test. They had an exam the next day, and the catch was it was 11 at night and the bus was leaving to drive down to Seattle from Vancouver, and then they would catch the flight to Mexico. The bus was leaving at 4 in the morning. Sam simply said, "I'm just going to go for it. Look, you know I will have a chance to fail exams many times in my college career, but I will only have a chance to go to Mexico for $200 once. I'm going to do it."

So he went for it. (He had a great time and still looks at pictures from that trip today.)

And when he went back to school after he returned, the instructor of the class said, "I noticed you weren't there for the exam" and Sam had already accepted that he had failed and would have to somehow make up for that. So he said to the professor, "Yeah I had to leave the country on some personal business."

The professor said, "You had to leave the country on personal business?"

"Yes I was out of the country."

"Well you can take the exam, then. I have an alternative copy of it. The questions are different, but the material it covers is the same."

Sam took the exam and passed it.

Fortune favors the bold. So take your dream out of dream status and take some action on it today. Not tomorrow.

53. Tap Into Cause and Effect

Shallow men believe in luck . . . strong men believe in
cause and effect.

Ralph Waldo Emerson

We find the biggest thing that holds people back from
creating any wealth in their life is their unwillingness to see
that they can actually *cause* things to happen. They don't
tap into the law of cause and effect.

They're expecting something to happen to them!

"When this situation happens *to* me...." they say. But
they don't see that they can be the *cause* of something good.

So they're always waiting. Hoping to get caught up in
something successful, or be in the right place at the right
time. They think, "If I can just catch the wave, it'll carry me
to the shore."

We tell clients who have big vision paralysis to start by
doing two things a week. That's it. Because two things a
week that you proactively do will move your vision from
the future into the present. Two things a week is 100 things
a year. If you do 100 conscious activities in a year, it's a
guarantee that you will *cause* something to happen.

Lack of activity, lack of attention, lack of investing thought into that subject causes it to stay out there. You can be the cause that activates the law of cause and effect.

Several days after the Indianapolis Colts beat the Chicago Bears in the 2007 Super Bowl, a rumor surfaced regarding a post-game congratulatory meeting between the winning quarterback Peyton Manning and Rex Grossman, quarterback of the Bears. Rex Grossman asked Peyton how he was able to so effectively grasp and throw the football in the variable, sometimes torrential rain conditions of that Sunday evening. (Rex Grossman himself had fumbled twice and threw interceptions at the game's critical junctures, attributing those results to the inclement conditions.) Peyton Manning had incurred a right-hand thumb injury in the AFC Championship Game that potentially would have been disastrous for his big game. Add that to the rain, and it was amazing that he was not affected. Peyton responded to Rex that he practiced "wet snaps" from center during the previous week and went on to say that because the ball was wet, he needed to lighten his grip to throw in the rain, which countered the tendency to grip the ball hard in such a game.

This rumored conversation was reported on ESPN Radio's Dan Patrick show. Tony Dungy, the Colts' winning coach, was a guest that day, and Dan could not resist asking if this rumor was true. Did the Colts really practice "wet snaps"? Tony assured the audience that any time during the season when an outdoor game might present wet conditions, Peyton Manning had 10 footballs soaked in water and practiced handling snaps and passing for hours.

See the contrast here between a person who chooses to *cause* success and someone who is at the effect of life. Rex Grossman was at the mercy of the weather. He went into the game hoping the bad weather wouldn't effect him too much, but, alas, bad luck, it did.

But Peyton Manning tapped into the power of *cause*. How can I *cause* a good result to happen? How can I *cause* effective ball handling in the rain? Well I'll just soak down some footballs and cause myself to be totally comfortable with that. I'll have those wet footballs snapped to me for hours so that my hands are used to them. I'll cause "wet" to feel normal. Rather than hoping the weather will be okay, I'll cause it to be okay.

Hope is not a strategy.

If you want something (like your prosperity) to be different than it looks like, ask yourself a useful question: how can I *cause* that to happen?

54. Sell Before You Build

Losing an illusion makes you wiser than finding a truth.

Ludwig Borne

There is an illusion that people who open small businesses are prone to believing and it says, "Build it and they will
come!"

This is what we call the "field of dreams" myth. Many
small business owners put all their work into getting their
doors open, getting their business physically and legally
ready for business, and then hoping for the best.

If you have done this, too, you have left out the most
important part of success: the unique, compelling, and cool
appeal of your business to customers!

What have you created that sets you apart? What are
you offering that has your customer say, "Wow! Cool!"
when they hear all about you? What's the urban legend
about your business? What's the buzz?

Once you've gotten yourself excited—and we mean
truly *excited* about your business—you're ready to do business. (Customers and prospective customers can't get excited if you're not.)

It's not enough to just open the doors and wait. You
need to add value to your offer. And you need to keep

doing this. Keep reinventing, over and over. Start your business over every Monday by asking (during your creative thinking time, the MOST IMPORTANT time you'll ever spend), *"What can I change or add to my product or service that will make this even more attractive and compelling and irresistible?"*

Most new business owners think in linear, logical order: "I'll get my customers after I open." But we are asking you to think backwards. Do some reverse engineering: start with the outcome you want and work backwards into the present moment so you can get your customers *before* you open.

Some health clubs have achieved mastery at this. Prior to their facility being ready, they will have a kiosk or desk in the mall open for months registering people into new memberships.

They know it's not true that all they have to do is "build it and they will come."

Another thing you can do to pre-sell the universe on your success is to personally go around to neighboring businesses and introduce yourself *before* your business is open. Make the first move. Show them what kind of person you are, caring for their businesses as much as you do your own. Start forming alliances early. Don't make them learn about you and just wonder about you, watching your new place get signs in the window, not knowing who you are. Get yourself out there so you can start telling your story early. Sell *before* you build.

Your whole goal is to sow the seeds of caring and quality ahead of time, even before you open. Introduce yourself to the community so you won't have to offer some kind of cut-rate "introductory" prices. Nine out of ten people don't buy on price, even when they say they do. They buy because you can solve their problems for them faster and in a more comfortable way than the competition. So remember: sell first—open second.

Think "PRE!" Pre-market, pre-sell, pre-mail, and pre-enroll people into being excited about your business when it opens. Do as much as you can ahead of time.

Sam has opened a small business in a small town where he pre-marketed and pre-publicized so dramatically that when the business was finally opened, it was a big community event! The mayor was there to cut a ribbon! (Mayors, being politicians, actually enjoy this kind of thing. And it gets you some nice coverage in the local papers.)

Remember the psychology of the customer in all of this. Customers make their buying decision long *before* any money changes hands. When you are buying your new car, your decision is made long before you sit down for the paperwork. Once you can picture yourself in that car, the sale is basically over.

So, give the world some pictures to live into before you open.

55. Invest Your Mental Energy

A single idea, the sudden flash of a thought, may be worth a
million dollars.

Robert Collier

When it comes down to wealth, the best thing you have
to invest is your mental energy. And if your mental energy
is distracted and put into worthless, toxic things, like argu-
ing with reality or judging what's going wrong in your life,
you are making a bad investment.

When you're lying in bed about to go to sleep at night,
are you thinking about your problems and bills you have
to pay, or are you thinking about potential opportunities?
When you're driving your car or just sitting around somewhere with nothing else to do or waiting in line at the
bank, what are you thinking about? Are you thinking in
terms of opportunity, or are you thinking in terms of
problems?

It's time now to really be careful about how your energy is channeled. And watch out for other people to make
sure that no one takes your mental energy in the wrong
direction.

If you have a business now and have an employee that's a real problem, put the energy into figuring out how to replace him with a great person. Not how to "deal with" this problem every day. (Good people are the greatest asset that you have.)

Nobel prize-winning scientist Linus Pauling said, "The best way to have a good idea is to have lots of ideas." But you can't have lots of ideas if you're not disciplined enough to focus on what you want. That's all discipline is, anyway—remembering what you want!

Begin to realize how very precious your mental energy and your attention are. That's why you use the phrase "pay attention" because you're *paying* (and investing) your attentive energy into some subject. Your attention is your wealth. So be aware of where it's being invested. Keep doing your gut checks throughout the day: Is this where I want my mental energy to go right now? Will it create wealth? Is it a high-return subject? Am I selling to high-probability buyers or low? If I put enough mental energy into this subject, will wealth return as a result? If the answer is No, then I want to just move along!

Move your mental energy into an area that will return something.

We're not saying to obsess 24 hours a day. But as long as you're "at work" why not do this?

The problem often is daily loss of focus. Massive leakage of mental energy. We think of a thousand different things.

Anything we focus on long enough comes into our life. When we think of one thing, that one thing will be drawn to us, so it is essential we maintain our focus on what we want.

56. Buy Some Happiness Now

But it is a pretty thing to see what money will do!

Marcus Annaeus Seneca

We've been told forever that money can't buy happiness.

Is that true? Maybe money can buy happiness. Not necessarily for ourselves, but for other people.

You can donate money to good causes, and by doing that you will actually make a difference in someone else's happiness level. If you build a well in Africa, you can increase the happiness level of the people in the village. If you help a family raise money for a medical treatment, you watch what money can do for happiness.

Someone telling you that "money can't buy happiness" is usually trying to put a heavy spin on their bitterness about money. When they say it can't buy happiness you might say, "Well, actually it can buy happiness for a lot of people, and that's why I feel great making it."

The Beatles sing that money "Can't Buy Me Love," but it can buy an expression of love for others. Former Phoenix Suns basketball player Kevin Johnson has put together a program in the schools where he grew up so that the kids aren't just on the streets all the time. Now they've got compelling school programs that they just love doing. And the kids are loving it, and they feel the love from the teachers. So Kevin Johnson's money is buying some love.

Wealth can buy you an expression of love going outward; it just can't buy you the receipt of love coming in. But who needs that anyway? We've all already got that inside; we were born with that.

57. Find Out That No One Is Coming

The best way to predict the future is to create it.

Peter Drucker

Daniel Pink has written a wonderful book about how many people are now in business for themselves called *Free Agent Nation*. Pink says, "We used to have a system in this country where companies offered employees security, and employees offered companies loyalty. That bargain has come undone. Anybody who still believes it is a fool."

One of the great breakthroughs in Steve's life was the work he did with psychotherapist and author Nathaniel Branden and his wife, the life coach Devers Branden.

Dr. Branden had an ongoing saying and theme he taught his clients to understand. The saying was this: "No one is coming." How powerful for you if you could just get that concept clearly in your mind and heart: No one is coming! No one is coming to live your life for you. No one is coming to solve your personal problems for you. No one is coming to attract your wealth for you.

No matter what you do, life is going to be about what you do with your life, and the wealth that you create. We're not saying don't use coaches and advisors and helpers. Just be aware that when they succeed, they succeed by connecting you to the best parts of yourself. By showing you what's inside you. It's back to you.

No one is coming to live your life for you. And no company can do that for you either. No spouse can do it (although people keep changing spouses, hoping it will happen if they can just get the right one.)

A lot of people are disappointed inside of companies because they keep thinking that Microsoft or IBM or Nokia or somebody "is going to be the final answer for me! They're going to provide that missing piece, which is my life direction."

It's almost an attempt for people to get childhood reinstated again and find a new form of parent. And you can't blame people for wanting that, because they were conditioned throughout childhood to think their parents would take care of them and look after them, and so don't worry about anything.

And then, boom, at 18 it's like, whoops, just kidding! It's all up to YOU! A lot of people feel shocked and betrayed by that and resent it and resist it. Then they go back out looking for new parents, subconsciously, and that's why they're so bitter about their company experience. Why they hate their supervisors.

You get that Dilbert anti-company effect because it just wasn't what they had hoped for: A second childhood. Someone coming!

But it's not bad news that no one is coming. It's good news. Because the ultimate source of wealth is in you. You'll do more to find your wealth by sitting alone in a room all day with just you and a blank pad of paper than you will with a hundred interactions with the world outside you. It's in you.

You will end up creating your own wealth in life, and you can do it, and it's not even all that hard.

Dr. Branden (www.nathanielbranden.com) tells the story of leading a group therapy session when someone spoke out and said, "Dr. Branden, you say that no one is coming, but that's not true. You came. You came into our lives and showed us how to live with higher and higher self-esteem. And our lives got better and better. So don't say no one is coming because you came."

"It's true," said Dr. Branden. "I did come. But I came to tell you that no one is coming."

58. Now Make Money Important

Money isn't everything,
as long as you have enough.

Malcolm Forbes

In the entertaining David Mamet movie *The Heist*, Danny DeVito's character famously says, "Everybody needs money. That's why they call it money!"

But people also always say, "Money isn't everything." And it's always people who don't have enough of it who say that. It's not people with lots of money saying that money isn't everything.

When it comes to the physical realm that we're in, unfortunately, in one sense, money *is* everything. Because every choice that you make in your physical nature is determined by how much money you have: where you're going to live, how often you get to see your kids, how much you get to see your wife, the experiences that you have with your family, and to a large degree how healthy you are. Studies have shown that people who have a higher income and have more money can actually live longer just because they have access to better medical care, to better ways of living and eating.

In his lively book *No B.S. Wealth Attraction for Entrepreneurs*, our friend and sometime mentor Dan Kennedy quotes millionaire rock star Gene Simmons from the band KISS, who gives his advice about how to live a successful life. "Be clear," said Simmons, "be truthful. Stand there proudly, unapologetically, unabashedly, and say, 'I love cash. It will get me everything I want in life.'"

How long you live is impacted by your money. So don't cop out and dismiss money by saying that money isn't everything.

And that's the paradox.

Because as we also said earlier, you'll make money faster when it's less important to you!

So the trick is to get it on both levels. Important and not important. Important enough to pay attention and focus and be mindful. Not important enough to stress out over.

The real problem with the "money isn't everything" philosophy is that people use it as a ticket to go unconscious. They start to stress over money; then they get scared and declare that it means nothing. To deal with the money stress they fog themselves over with food, alcohol, illicit relationships, television, gambling, and family disagreements. All of those ridiculous addictions are designed to generate fog and loss of consciousness.

The thinking is this: If I can get everyone to agree that money isn't everything and it's only money, then I can go unconscious about my own creation of wealth in life, and it's my ticket out of the game. And I don't have to feel responsible for the fact that I'm not a player.

But you *do* want to play the game. Because the great and gentle game of wealth is a fun game to play. And like any other fun game it has to be played with a high degree of consciousness and recognition. It's time to recognize that money, in the physical realm, is good to have. Because when you see that wealth determines what clothing you wear, what car you drive, what food you eat, and the retreats you go on, then you're more excited in a good way—and you can bring more of yourself to the game of creating wealth for your life.

Many people never allow themselves the joy of succeeding at what they do. They get so tangled up in fears, complaints, and resentments that they don't see how clear a shot they have at being extremely successful. Don't let this happen to you. Realize this: you can serve and help many more people if you are successful than if you are not. It is not ego or greed driving successful people; it's a pure love of life itself. Allow yourself that pleasure.

The great and successful novelist W. Somerset Maugham had it right when he said, "The common idea that success spoils people by making them vain, egotistic, and self-complacent is erroneous; on the contrary, it makes them, for the most part, humble, tolerant, and kind. Failure makes people bitter and cruel."

59. Set the Valve to IN

As long as you keep yourself centered,
and are fulfilling the purpose you were sent here for,
you will succeed and be prosperous in all areas of life.

Jose Silva

There is a natural flow to money.

There's a psychological version of this flow that we all have. And if we make the determination that money flows in, and that's the primary movement of the flow, it will actually happen that way. But it has to be a conscious intention.

Some people talk about their own psychological cash flow by saying, "I never seem to hold onto money." Or: "How is it that I'm always broke? It just keeps on flying out faster than it's flying in."

In most Chinese restaurants and Chinese stores you can find a little ceramic cat that's holding up one paw. Next time you go into a Chinese restaurant, you'll see that ceramic cat; almost all of them have it. It will usually be right next to the cash register. It's the good fortune cat, and it means "money comes in." Wealth cats, also famously known as beckoning cats, are now enjoying wonderful popularity with all shop owners around the world! This colorful symbol of wealth originated in Japan. Soon China took notice and made the wealth cats their own because of their psychological potency. They actually alter the flow of money.

Money comes in. And seeing the cat helps the mind tune itself to "in." But, that's silly, isn't it?

Maybe not. Have you seen what's happening with China lately? Their whole nation's cash flow valve is set for "in." Basically the cat is just a little symbol, but it's a powerful psychological trigger for "money comes in."

You can create just such a trigger in you. You can always be thinking of cash flowing in. "Cash comes into my life; it doesn't just go out of my life." (We become what we think about.)

When you use the affirmation "cash flows in" for a while, it becomes more than an affirmation. It's soon living deeper in your mind as an operating principle. It has made its neural pathway there inside the spongy receptive brain. If you work on it and let it permeate into your decision making, it can guide you.

When you have a determination to set the valve to "in" rather than to "out," it can help you make decisions. Do you want to buy this new vehicle right now? In the back of your mind, you hear, "Well, that would be having the valve on 'out' if I did that." Therefore, the answer is no for the moment.

So something that started as an affirmation ends up as an operating principle inside your system, and that's where it really gets powerful. Neutral situations start to show up as more opportunities for cash flowing in because your mind has been programmed now to see them.

60. Succeed by Failing

Failure is the foundation of success and the means
by which it is achieved.

Lao-tzu

Most people want to succeed by succeeding, which
makes sense.

But when failure happens, it can be the best teacher
ever. We realize that we're free to experiment more. And as
Dale Dauten says in his classic little business book *The Max
Strategy*, "Experiments never fail."

Sam had five straight business failures before he turned
it all around. These 100 ways in this book represent the
exact changes he made to execute the turnaround and
become a millionaire. They not only worked for him, but
they have worked for his hundreds of clients who have
transformed failure to success.

But he later found that all the failures he had were also
helping the successes happen in retrospect. By paying close
attention to their lessons, they were paying off.

Some people just look at failure as failure. But failure
can actually help you develop skills. The great quarterback
Fran Tarkenton wrote a book called *What Losing Taught Me
about Winning* that described how he had drawn from his

losses on the football field to help him succeed as a business person after his sports career was over.

Sam says, "Some people ask, 'How do you overcome the fear of business failure?' I just say, 'Fail a couple of times and you won't be afraid of it.'"

Failure is just information. It tells you what's working and what's not working. Your success is sped up by information on what it is in life that doesn't work, because the more of that you can learn, the sooner you're getting to what *does* work.

We got an email from Matt Furey (you can get his emails, too, and we recommend them at www.mattfurey.com) in which he said,

> This evening I sat in the sauna with my son, Frank, talking about what it takes to get good at anything. He's only six, but he's primed and ready for knowledge on how to build a powerful self-image.
>
> "Could you tell me about something you didn't used to be able to do?" I asked. "Something that used to be hard for you but now it's easy."
>
> "Throwing a football," he immediately said.
>
> "Okay, what else?"
>
> "Catching a football."
>
> "And ...?"
>
> "Punching and kicking."
>
> "Okay, great. Can you think of anything else?"
>
> "Hmmm, I guess writing."
>
> "Any idea how many things you've forgotten? How about learning to roll over, to crawl, to stand, to walk, to run, to get dressed, to feed yourself, and so on."
>
> Frank's eyes went wide with wonder.
>
> "All of these things were once very difficult for you. You struggled with them. You made a ton of mistakes. Yet now you can do them a lot, lot easier, right?"
>
> "Right."

"Do you know what this means?" I asked. "It means that anything you want to learn, the same rules will apply. At first you'll make mistakes. You'll struggle. Then you'll make fewer mistakes because the mistakes are teaching you WHAT to do. Then, if you pay attention like you have so far, you'll be able to do the new thing, too. It's as simple as that. But if you whine and complain and cry about your mistakes, you'll never get anywhere. You'll think poorly about yourself and you'll get results that don't make you happy."

Matt said, "I talked with Frank for 15 minutes about the value mistakes have in life—and I'll be reinforcing this talk over and over again. Of course, this is only a lesson for six-year old kids. I don't know of a single adult who could benefit from this knowledge. HA. All of us can. Don't fear mistakes. Use them as the corrective feedback they truly are. Mistakes lead to greatness—but only if you stop judging them as bad."

You can certainly succeed right off, and that's great when you do. But you'll still always have little failures after that. It is important to learn to make friends with those. You may have personnel failures, partnering failures, some product failures, or some expansion you tried that failed. Learn from them.

Make failure available to you as a teacher. Failure is the greatest teacher there is! You don't seek it, you don't want it, you're operating as if you're trying not to have it, but once it arrives, welcome it.

61. Find Someone with a Problem

The more difficult a problem becomes, the more interesting it is.

Andrew Carnegie

Money is like a chess game in which the object of the game is to take certain pieces off the board and clear a path to completion. And those pieces are best thought of as *other people's problems*.

Do you want the surest route to creating wealth? Find someone with a problem and solve that problem!

Maybe their problem is that there is old furniture in their yard that is too big to fit in their car to be taken away—take it away and let them pay you! You have solved their problem.

A client of ours recently paid us a large fee to help her solve her problem of poor sales figures for her business. We were able to apply principles we know about transforming sales failure and her problem was solved.

We were coaching a business consultant named Charles who wanted help with "marketing" himself.

"I need to market my consulting business better. I need some brochures, and a better presence on the internet and maybe a promotional DVD and a system for cold-calling. Can you help?"

"Sure. But, why do you want all that marketing material?"

"So I can market."

"Why do you think you need to market?"

"Doesn't everybody? To get new clients!"

"And exactly why do you want new clients?"

"To grow my business."

"To what end?"

"To make money! I don't see what you're driving at here!"

"What if you could get that money from existing clients and the people they refer? Then you could eliminate all those other costly steps—steps that usually don't work anyway."

Charles was like most people who always think they need *new* business and *new* clients and *new* money. They can't see that the fastest way to build wealth is through existing relationships that have already been created. They try to reinvent the wheel and start all over by chasing after strangers all day. They think it's smart marketing to do that. They can't see that it's weak marketing because the activity isn't solving anyone's problem.

We asked Charles, "How many past and current clients do you have?"

"About 15 I would say," said Charles, who hadn't been consulting for long.

"The fastest way to wealth is through those 15 people. Call them and listen. Visit them. Allow them to talk. Allow them to tell you their problems and troubles. Take notes. Ask questions. Truly understand their problems."

"That's all?"

"No. You are then going to sit with their problems and create potential solutions. Your solutions will be converted into proposals you make to them. You will solve their problems for them. The fastest way to create wealth for your consulting business is to find someone with a problem and solve it."

"What about marketing?"

"Solve enough problems and you'll never need it. They'll refer other people to you who also have problems."

People start their day wondering how to make more money. That's a futile approach. They would make more money if they started their day searching for other people's problems.

62. Play 20 Questions

A successful economy depends on the proliferation of the rich,
on creating a large class of risk-taking men and women who are
willing to shun the easy channels of a comfortable life in order
to create new enterprise, win huge profits, and
invest them again.

George Gilder

Even if you are not in business right now, it makes sense to ask every business person that you interact with how he or she does it. Ask about the market, how their business works, frustrations in their business, great points about their business—just to know.

Sam says, "A lot of the progress I've made in my business has been by asking other people questions about how they do things and seeing whether it's a good thing they're doing, a bad thing they're doing—and what can I learn from this? And even people in businesses that aren't doing well, it's instructive to get information from them."

Sam remembers talking to someone who ran a health food store a few years ago, and unfortunately they were stuck in the whole victim mode of "there's nothing I can do." Sam just started asking them about the health food business. And the owner started telling him countless stories about how the grocery stores are all starting to carry health food right now, so it was really tough to compete. He didn't see that there was a huge opportunity to do things like home delivery and focus on the one part of the market that grocery stores couldn't focus on.

"This was right around the same time that we had a company delivering fresh organic produce to our house every week," said Sam, "And that was their unique service. But there was no one in the local market doing it. And I was wondering why this guy couldn't deliver organic produce and have a shop-at-home service and do things that the big grocery stores won't do. So visiting with him was stimulating, even though he was failing."

You can always activate the cross-pollination effect. Other businesses are doing things that your business might not be doing and no one in your industry is doing. Even when you go to your association meetings or your franchise meetings, you read your industry magazine or look on your industry website, it's never there. But it's being done over there in a *different* industry, and if you'd apply it to yours, you'd have a breakthrough. That's why asking questions at every business you visit will lead to wealth and inspiration.

Checking into hotels on his speaking tours, Steve would always ask the managers questions. He found out that some hotel chains had looked at how airlines gave out frequent flier miles and decided to do their own "frequent visitor" programs with benefits to customer loyalty. They could have looked for decades at their own industry and never found that idea.

These kinds of things come up when you play *20 questions* with other business owners that you talk to. (There is a warning, however, when you play this game: don't believe them when they start talking about all the things that are holding them back from success. Don't get lured into that. You don't want to catch that victim virus. When you talk to a business owner with a lot of victim stories, be sure to wash your hands before leaving.)

By asking questions everywhere you go, you can't help but learn. And as the great motivational teacher Jim Rohn says, "Learning is the beginning of wealth. Learning is the beginning of health. Learning is the beginning of spirituality. Searching and learning is where the miracle process all begins."

63. Don't Seek Money Up Front

When you have exhausted all possibilities, remember this—you haven't.

Thomas Edison

We don't want to come across like we're saying, "Get rich while you sleep, with no money down!" But the truth is you don't need money to make money.

There was a review of our *9 Lies* book in a newspaper that said, "One of the lies kind of tries to stretch it a bit, because it says you should treat your customers well and use the Open Hand and spend money on them, but then it also says that you don't need money to make money! But if you don't need money to make money, where are you going to get money to spend on your customers?"

By selling your service! (Maybe that's why newspapers are going out of business.)

Most successful businesses today were started with a very small amount of money. If any! Larry Farrell is a leading expert on entrepreneurial behavior, and he says a typical startup business now starts with less than $12,000. And a majority of small business starts now are actually financed by people using a single credit card to do so!

A lot of our coaching clients go into various forms of consulting: health care consulting, personal training consulting, life coaching consulting, all different kinds of consulting. (Some of them took Tom Peters' advice to "Quit the company you're working for and let them hire you back as a consultant!") The way they start their business is not by finding money and then opening an office. They start by finding a client!

Then they sit down and negotiate with the client for a pre-payment for a year's worth of services, and that's their seed money. It's from an existing client. So you need clients to make money, you need customers to make money; you don't need money to make money.

One of the people we were advising recently had no credit, or bad credit, and she needed to get a certain amount of money to make the jump from running a small, part-time business out of her house to an actual commercial space. Finally she offered her clients a pre-pay arrangement where they would pay for a year in advance. And of course, she was borrowing from herself, but it was better than not being able to borrow at all. So the whole "I need money to make money" approach is just wrong.

You just need to be willing to *sell* to make money. Because that's how the money's going to be made, anyway.

You might as well do it up front!

If it's unearned money you get from an investor, who knows if you can actually turn it into more? But if you have the ability to sell the initial clients on paying you that money, then you can definitely do well. Earned money is stronger than borrowed or invested money every time.

64. Win By One Stroke

We evolve not by dreaming of giant steps,
but by committing ourselves in action to little ones,
moving step by relentless step in an ever-expanding
field of vision.

Nathaniel Branden

In golf, if you win by one stroke, you can get millions of dollars in prize money. But for second place you'll just get a fraction of that.

A single stroke is all it takes in life, too. A lot of people become preoccupied and think it takes so much more. They think they have to be much, much better than everyone else to succeed.

But the truth is, you just have to win by one stroke.

One gentle little swing, and you're in. You just have to be slightly preferred by your customer over someone else. And the same is true if you work in an organization and want that promotion. You just have to be slightly preferred over the other person. And you can be preferred by one small stroke. That one stroke of courtesy or kindness you put into your work that others don't, and you win.

It's the small differences you make that catapult you ahead. While others struggle to succeed, always thinking of the differences they would like to make but can't, you can win. Just move to the differences you can make. The smaller the better.

Billionaire Warren Buffet says the reason he succeeded financially was, "I didn't look to jump over seven-foot bars; I looked around for one-foot bars that I could step over."

65. Choose One Thing to Do

He who makes time precious lives forever.

Peter Megargee Brown

Winning by one stroke means managing your time, so that when you stand over the ball there's nothing in your mind but that one stroke.

That's what they say separates Tiger Woods from the rest of the field. When the rest of the field stands over a ball, they think of 10 different things. How far behind am I? Is this really the right club? How can I forget that last bad hole?

Tiger is different.

He's just doing one thing.

He's just putting a good shot on the ball he's hitting right now. That's it. (The ultimate life management system.)

Many people in this chaotic, fast-paced world ask us to coach them on time management. How do I manage my time better? How do I get everything done? What can I do when I have too much to do? The ultimate time management system (the one Tiger uses) is to just hit the ball you're standing over.

Thomas Merton was a monk, theologian, poet and author of more than 50 books before his young life was cut short by an accidental electrocution. He ironically died by trying to do two things at once, stepping out of a bath tub and adjusting a poorly-grounded electric fan.

But his beautiful spiritual books live on today. We love Merton's quotation on this subject of doing too much:

> "To allow oneself to be carried away by a multitude of conflicting concerns, to surrender to too many demands, to commit oneself to too many projects, to want to help everyone in everything is to succumb to violence. More than that, it is cooperation in violence. The frenzy of the activist neutralizes his work for peace. It destroys his own inner capacity for peace. It destroys the fruitfulness of his own work, because it kills the root of inner wisdom which makes work fruitful."

Steve will never forget the woman who came up to him in one of his seminars. She had a copy of *Reinventing Yourself*, which had been passed out to everyone in the room and she said, "I'm really offended by the title of this book, *Reinventing Yourself*."

And Steve said, "How does it offend you?"

She said, "Well, it makes me think that there's something wrong with me—that I have to reinvent myself. Why should I have to think that? Why do I always have to fix myself? Do I really?"

"No, of course you don't. And when you read the book, you'll see that the book itself is based on the premise that people reinvent themselves *faster* when they have the courage to see that there's *nothing* wrong with them. Nothing whatsoever. That's the first step in joyful reinvention."

Most people come in to our coaching conversations and training seminars with a laundry list of things that they think are wrong with them including numerous personal limitations. Therefore, (and this is a hard thing for people to see,) when they have the courage to really admit, deep down, that there's nothing wrong with them whatsoever, that's when they take off. That's when they can reinvent themselves in a newly prosperous way.

Eleanor Roosevelt said, "No one can make me feel inferior without my permission." That's ownership. That's owning your own spirit and that's the key to time management!

In any given moment we are either owners or victims. Ownership is high consciousness—we can see the big picture. While victimization, on the other hand, has us being victims of circumstance. Soon we're overwhelmed with too many things to do. We don't have time to do them.

But when we're in the ownership position, we're in a position, mentally, to utilize the ultimate time management system of doing one thing and only one. When we're in a victim position, we feel overwhelmed and swamped.

The victim says, "I'm swamped, I'm overwhelmed. The world is asking too much of me. Don't people know I only have 24 hours in a day? I've got way too much to do and not enough time to do it!"

Here's the irony. Let's say you take the victim thinking position (which always leads to fatigue, another irony) and you're sitting there trying to do a task. Let's say your next task is to call Joseph and talk to him about an upcoming project. In your mind (if you're a victim) you're thinking, "I've got to call Joseph, but I've also got about 50 other things to do and at least three things to do within the next 20 minutes, but I'm going to call Joseph anyway. So, when I call him I've got three things in the back of my mind that will keep coming to the front of my mind while I'm talking to him."

Now Joseph is talking to you. And you're talking and taking a few notes, and then Joseph says something to you but your mind has drifted to another of the three things you have to do in the next 20 minutes. You're not really focusing, and you and he are not advancing anything forward, and finally you're both kind of frustrated and you both say, "Hey, let's talk later. Let's get this done at another time. It looks like we need to talk a little more about this and why don't we talk next week? Maybe if we talk closer to the event we could get more done, but I'll e-mail you—why don't you e-mail me—here's my e-mail address and I'll get back to you later, and I'll send you some things and we'll move this forward later."

That conversation—because it was not complete—was a waste of your time. All because you weren't focusing when you talked.

Now you've postponed what you were going to do in this conversation (and this kind of incomplete activity happens all day!). You had so many things going on in your mind that you couldn't relax into a conversation with Joseph in such a way that you got total closure on what you are doing.

And now the new, future conversation with Joseph has entered the queue of all these things you have unfinished and left to do. It takes a number and gets in line in your mind (where the lines go around the block now.) Now you'll walk around with the thought of "I need to finish this up with Joseph" in the back of your mind all day, which robs you of energy and makes your next task also very likely to be incomplete—very likely to suffer the same fate that your conversation with Joseph suffered.

Soon all your activities go this way: totally fragmented, lopsided, unfinished, not beautiful, not relaxed, but just a kind of a ragged attempt to *get through* a conversation.

We've isolated this one conversation because it's very typical of what we do throughout the day. This can happen 50 times a day when we come from the victim perspective. Especially from thinking, "I'm swamped; I'm overwhelmed; I have way too much to do." This victim perspective is the ultimate ineffective time management system. Even if you have long lists of tasks and all sorts of things to delegate, it's still a mess because the chaos is in your own mind, not on paper. The chaos is in your brain.

And that's what it looks like on the outside too! In a world of running around trying to get all this done.

There is another way.

There is another system, and that's the system that we call "One thing to do." The ultimate time management system is to only have one thing to do, ever. To simply stand over that golf ball and before you put a good stroke on it, know that it's all you have to do. And you'll be a winner.

People say, "One thing to do!?! Well, that would be nice!"

But let's really slow this down and look at it. Remember a time when you had a vacation day and woke up and only had one thing to do that day? You got up out of bed and maybe the one thing to do was to go to the store and buy a card. You were going to buy a birthday card for someone that day and put it in the mail, but that was the only thing you had to do. Picture how that felt. Picture how beautiful that was—luxurious, relaxed, wonderful, almost like you owned the world. There's just one thing to do! You can go get that birthday card on your own sweet time. So you have a leisurely breakfast, you sit and look out over the water, and you take a little walk; and when you're good and ready, you get in the car and go to the market. Then you go to the card store and browse for a while and think about your friend whose birthday it is. Soon you find a really funny but thoughtful card that you know your friend will like. It reminds you of something that he and you shared a long time ago. You drive home and write out very carefully a little message to your friend in the card—something that's touching, something he'll get a kick out of. You put the card in the envelope, address it, put a stamp on it, and put it out next to the front door on the little bookshelf by the front door. You know it will get mailed tomorrow and so your task is over. You've done your one thing.

Maybe a week from now you'll get a call from your friend who says, "Boy that card was great; it was so funny; it was just wonderful to get it. Thanks for taking the time to get it; it was so thoughtful of you," and your friendship's enhanced and it feels very good. Doing one thing tends to turn out that way.

What if we could live every day this way? What if every day we only had one thing to do? How beautiful would life be? What if our conversation with Joseph was the only thing we had to do back on that day when it was so diffuse and frantic?

Let's rewind and look at what that conversation would have been like played over again. You're about to call Joseph, this time you get some notes together, pull some files down, print out a few e-mails, and then you're sitting there with them in front of you feeling well-organized. You take a breath before the call and think a little bit about it. You sit in an easy chair, call up Joseph, and ask him if he really has time to talk right now.

Joseph says, "Sure."

You say, "Great, let's go over this. Let's make sure we finish this up so there's nothing more to do."

Joseph says, "That would be a wonderful thing."

In a very relaxed way, you go through all you want to discuss. You listen very carefully to him, and you're only thinking about this conversation. It's the only thing in the world for you. It's the only thing that exists. You relax so thoroughly into it that you and he come up with some really good ideas. When you hang up you feel great. Just like you feel when you've made a clean hit on the ball. One stroke. You get up from your chair ready for what's next. Whatever that is. You know it will be the only thing you have to do that day.

Pick one thing and do it well. Just one thing. Full focus, full charm, full creativity, tie it up in a ribbon and send it off as a gift well-done. Then step into your next thing. Maybe your next thing is nothing. Just the breath you take before your next thing, or the prayer of thanks you offer for being alive to do these things one at a time. Maybe your next thing is 10 minutes of planning the future. Soon your future will evolve and emerge like a beautiful flower. People are rewarded for how they do their one thing, not for how many things they worry about.

66. Don't Get Your Act Together

Once I drew like Raphael but it has taken me a lifetime to
draw like a child.

Pablo Picasso

Evangeline wanted to offer her services as a trainer to a
large organization whose president she met at her children's preschool. His company was one of the largest in the
state; and she knew that if she could get a contract there,
she would be set for a long time.

But she was upset when she called. She said, "I can't
approach Mr. Johanson, I don't have my act together yet. I
can't get myself to go in to see him."

"That puts you in a good position!"

"What do you mean?"

"You can show up as a real person. You can go in right
away with a more charming approach. Just call and say,
'I've got to tell you I don't have my act together, but I want
to meet with you. I don't know what I am doing, I may be
insane, this thing I'm going to ask of you, you might throw
me out of the office. But all I need is 15 minutes of your
time.'"

"Wow. What do I do when I get there?"

"You might say, 'I have no idea how to say this, so I'm just going to blurt it out. I've got the skills and experience to train all of your people, and I can make a huge difference in productivity for you. What I'm requesting is one paid pilot session with you in the room as a witness and what I can promise is that I won't waste a minute of your time.'"

Evangeline said nothing.

"Look, are you committed to serving that person?"

She said, "Oh, yeah. I'll serve him till the end of his days".

"Great, just go tell him that and start from there. You don't have to have your act together yet. This is not about artificial manipulation. Just connect. Make your best connection on a human level, no matter how charmingly awkward, and then get inside and go."

Evangeline lit up. Previously she had believed that one always had to have things prepared to perfection before ever asking for anything that involved money. But people are in a hurry. That CEO Mr. Johanson she met would appreciate the speed with which she showed up in his office.

She took her chance and went right in to see him. She was willing to be vulnerable and real. His heart melted at her enthusiasm for what she could do for his people. He gave her immediate permission to set up the pilot.

Evangeline said, "I'm really happy that I'm getting to do the pilot. It was hard to walk in and do that without a lot of detailed preparation, but it was just my energy that won him over."

You don't have to always have your act together. You don't always need a polished technique or script. Just trust the basic childish innocence of authentic commitment to serve. Trust that a deep desire to serve someone will always connect, no matter how you say things.

As the great German philosopher-poet Goethe said, "Once you learn to trust yourself you will know how to live."

67. Let Someone Else Do Your Homework

Formal education will make you a living.
Self-education will make you a fortune.

Jim Rohn

A lot of people jump into a risky wealth opportunity that they are happy to do by trial and error. Then they fall on their face and wonder what happened.

They don't realize that a lot of other people went down that path before, and they know where it ends up. They now know what to do and what not to do.

So it can be extremely useful to your wealth curve to prowl and troll and study websites and articles about successful businesses similar to yours in your category. Because people, when they succeed, get excited about how they succeeded. They want to share what they did and what they know. Look through what other people have on their websites. What kind of things do they offer? What do they charge for it? How does it work?

They've done the homework already.

If you come across someone who's successful, ask them questions, and they will tell you how they did it.

Sam, who owns music and dance studios, was at a seminar once that was full of karate studio owners. He had learned pretty much all the things he could learn from the music and dance studio market, so he wanted to look at a karate studio seminar and see what they knew that he could possibly use. They went around the room and attendees were asked to say how many students they had and what their gross sales were to introduce themselves. And everyone is saying, I have 150 students, I have 100, I have 300, I've got 250, all the typical numbers. And it got around to Sam and he said, "I've got 3,000."

And everyone just kind of looked at him.

You'd think that the first break that came up, everyone would run over to him and say, "What are you doing? How are you doing this? Are you doing direct marketing?" But they didn't say a word. It was a room full of karate studio owners and they were so testosterone-driven and egotistical that they thought, "Well, what can this dance studio guy tell me?"

Sam said, "And they were all sitting there thinking, "Well, I can beat the **** out of this guy! That's why I don't care if he's more successful than me."

But Sam was thinking, "I can pay those five guys there to beat the **** out of you, so...who's more dangerous?"

Let go of the egocentric thinking that says you have to use your own genius to succeed. Stop it with, "If I didn't come up with the idea, then it's not my idea; so what! That doesn't mean it isn't a great idea for me to use."

It's ego that stops people from letting someone else do their homework. But when you're more committed to success than you are to looking good, you'll get your ideas anywhere you can find them. When you're making your deposit at the bank, the bank doesn't care if you did all the work yourself, or if someone else helped you. They put the money in your account just as quickly either way.

68. Think Open Hand

A man there was, and they called him mad;
the more he gave, the more he had.

John Bunyan

If who you are is good, give yourself. If your product is good, give someone the experience of it. Don't be stingy. Keep giving. Because what you give, you get.

If you have a natural tendency to think in terms of scarcity, you'll shut down the inflow of wealth by choking off the outflow. As you're more able to invest in your people and give yourself to the world, you'll let the money flow in and flow out, and you'll move to wealth much faster.

There is a segment in *9 Lies* where we briefly describe the Owner-Victim syndrome. And because there was an entire book written previously about it (*Reinventing Yourself*), we just told the reader to email us for a free copy of that book if they wanted to read deeper on the subject. We just opened our hand and offered it. No hidden motive.

Many people have emailed us to take advantage of the offer, and we simply gave them the book. (We have received more coaching and seminar business from doing that one act than we ever intended up front.) We just wanted to give.

But it always comes back.

As the great Russian spiritual teacher Gurdjieff said, "If you help others, you will be helped. Perhaps tomorrow, perhaps in 100 years, but you will be helped. Nature must pay off the debt. It is a mathematical law and all life is mathematical."

69. Decide to Join the Millions of Millionaires

There is no defined limit as to how much money you can acquire in what little time. If any definition exists it does so just in your mind and in your emotions.

Stuart Wilde

In the 1950s it was a big fantasy dream to be a millionaire. They even had a show called *The Millionaire* about a rich and powerful man who was a super-hero because he was a millionaire!

The term "millionaire" and the connotation haven't really changed, but the ease of getting there certainly has.

The world has changed. For the better. A hundred years ago if we talked about going to Europe from the U.S., it would be a pretty arduous journey. You'd take a boat and it would be lengthy and hard. But now, even though Europe is in the same place and the U.S. is in the same place, the ease of getting back and forth has been simplified by 100 times. The cost is even 10 times less than it was. But a lot of people still have a psychological barrier, so they've never been to Europe. They've never been to Spain.

Sam was approached by someone recently who said to him, "Wow, you're a millionaire!? Wow!"

Sam recalls, "As I took my monocle off and blew some steam on it and rubbed it against my waist coat I said... 'The truth is it's not really as big a deal as it sounds. I'd like to build the mystique, but a lot of people can do it. There are millions and millions of millionaires. So it definitely can happen to you; don't think it's a far off, never-never land goal.'"

The old television show *The Millionaire* was popular on black and white TV. In the show the main hero was a *millionaire*, and because he was a millionaire, it seemed like he had unlimited wealth. In every episode, he'd decide to come into some dire situation where somebody was financially struggling and give the people money to bail them out. The suggestion was that maybe there's only one millionaire! There's only one Superman, only one Lone Ranger and there's only one Millionaire.

It was this same mystique of a million dollars that Mike Myers made fun of in *Austin Powers*, when Dr. Evil puts his finger to his cheek and says, "We will ask them for—ONE *MIL–LION* DOLLARS*!*" And the joke was that it was way too little of a ransom to ask for if you're going to blow up the whole world. And everyone just howled with laughter. And the whole joke was how little money that really has become.

A million is just a small number now.

One of the fastest tracks to becoming a millionaire is to not have that numerical mystique mean anything intimidating to you. You're a millionaire. So what? Are you fulfilled and having fun? That's what really matters. (And, ironically, that's usually the road to becoming a millionaire.)

70. Don't Get Hooked on Win-Win

If you limit your choices only to what seems possible or reasonable, you disconnect yourself from what you truly want, and all that is left is compromise.

Robert Fritz

The point here is to stop trying to "help" everyone by discounting your fee and giving them a "deal."

The win for them is already there if you have a great service. You don't have to add a new win on top of that win.

If who you are is great, they have already won by sitting down with you. You don't have to add to their win by cutting some deal with them and helping them out financially. If you're in a negotiation for any contracted services, you don't have to keep pushing money over to the other side of the table to help them out, and then cover it with thinking you're trying to go for a "win-win."

Because if what you have is valuable, they've already won. They're coming in with a win; you don't have to add to that. You need to stand proud and allow yourself to win, too, because they've already won just because they're doing business with you.

Jim Camp, in our opinion America's greatest negotiation coach, who wrote the masterpiece *Start With No*, insists that good negotiators avoid win-win. It makes better sense for both parties (and it guarantees better service) when you always sell yourself for what you're really worth.

In most cases "win-win" should be re-labeled as "I chickened out" and just gave them a deal because I really "needed" to make it. I caved. I linked money to survival. I thought it was a need. "Win-win" is usually code for "wuss-wuss."

MY WAGE

I bargained with Life for a penny,
And Life would pay no more,
However I begged at evening
When I counted my scanty store;

For Life is a just employer,
He gives you what you ask,
But once you have set the wages,
Why, you must bear the task.

I worked for a menial's hire,
Only to learn, dismayed,
That any wage I had asked of Life,
Life would have paid.

--J.B. Rittenhouse

71. Think Making Before Saving

I think that much of the advice given to young people about
saving money is wrong. I never saved a cent until I was forty
years old. I invested in myself—in study, in mastering my tools,
in preparation. Many a man who is putting a few dollars a
week into the bank would do much better to put it into himself.

Henry Ford

P eople can obsess with guilt about saving money.

They can spend huge amounts of time and energy
going through the weekly grocery store coupons, the
inserts, to figure out how they can save four to five
dollars.

All that energy could have been spent creating
money—calling forth wealth from the universe.

We're not saying you should be a fool about things and
pay more than you have to. But the exercise of saving,
hoarding, and clinging as your primary wealth objective is
dangerous on a couple of levels.

First of all, it makes you believe in scarcity. It anchors
lack in your belief system. There are only 100 marbles, so I
have to make sure I don't give away too many of those,

because there's only a set amount. So I have to watch every single marble that goes out.

I don't want to lose my marbles.

The second thing it does is distract you from the bigger opportunity, which is making money. We have a friend we will call Warren who's a consultant. He's got a nice regular executive job, and he also consults on the side. And he makes an average of $400 an hour consulting. Warren consults with large organizations and individuals alike. But it is nothing for him to spend two hours on the weekend trying to find where to get grass seed for five dollars less than where he's now getting it. He will look at grass seed at one place and spend the rest of the morning driving to four other places. And then when he gets one for five dollars less, he just cheers with delight, saying "*I have just saved us five dollars!*"

If he had spent one of those lost hours consulting on the phone, he'd be up by $395. But he doesn't see that. His emotions about the scarcity of money are keeping him from abundance. Even if he spent that hour with his little daughter instead of racing from store to store, he'd bring a happier Warren to his work hours next week and be even more successful.

And maybe it's fun for him to find that five-dollar savings, and maybe that plays into some deep psychological wound about money. But we suggest that Warren still has a scarcity mindset running his life that blinds him to his unlimited wealth.

Human beings are creators of wealth or they are not. (And this whole book is about how to shift from reacting to *creating.*) Therefore it is not a very smart activity for your brain to spend half a day chasing down five dollars.

When we pointed out to Warren that he could make a lot more money than he was saving he said, "Yeah, but you can't just do work all the time."

Well that's true, and if you're going to save money for the fun and satisfaction of it and you know that's all you're doing, then that's hard to oppose. But Warren wasn't doing his grass seed crusade in a very lighthearted way. He was serious. You could see the veins standing out on his neck as he drove from one mall to another. Warren was full of stress and anxiety until he found something cheaper.

Sam's family has a lady that comes in and cleans every week. When people ask them, "Wow, how do you afford to do that?" Sam replies, "It would cost me a lot more *not* to have a cleaning lady. House cleaning is a lot cheaper than marriage counseling. To make it a smart move financially, we just have to figure out how to get paid more per hour than I'm paying out for cleaning."

72. Focus on People with Money

It is not enough to be busy, so are the ants.
The question is, what are we busy about?

Henry David Thoreau

Recent reports have showed that 20 percent of the people in North America have 47 percent of the disposal income. That means that there are one in five people who really don't have to be concerned with your price if they don't want to be. They can purchase something from you if they want to.

If you are going to set up a business, or offer a service, don't forget that you can focus your service on that very type of customer. Many people don't realize that!

People we coach will often say, "Well, I have to be fair to the whole market picture, don't I? Don't I want the whole market to have access to what I do?"

Why? Are you a public service? Are you the government? Do you really have to be accessible to every single person?

If you're looking to sell yourself or your great product, you may as well go where the money is. It's harder to get money from people who don't have it.

While coaching Caroline, who just opened up a practice as a fitness trainer, we asked her to describe her ideal client to us. Where does he live? How old is he? How often would he come in? What does he like?

"I don't know," Caroline said. "I don't care. I just need clients."

Wrong answer. Caroline failed to see that she could be as creative and intelligent about finding the right clients as she was about developing her fitness expertise. Finally, after we spent some sessions helping her decide who her ideal client would be, Caroline had a number of break-throughs and exciting ideas about how to jump start her business. She started with her ready-made client list and created a powerful referral program that eliminated the need to advertise, market, network, or schmooze.

By focusing on people who had greater likelihood of using and affording her services, she bypassed all the trouble people encounter when they're "always open for anybody." You can do the same.

73. Think Small

Be faithful in small things because it is in them that
your strength lies.

Mother Teresa

Remember that bigger is not better. Bigger is just bigger.

Our friend, and here we'll call him Pierre, was the head
of a group of information technology trainers. They
worked out of a small rented office with very little over-
head, and they were successful training major companies
in I.T.

But soon Pierre had the urge to get bigger. Expansion
for the sake of expansion. Isn't that how the big boys do it?
He started plotting the purchase of a massive building.
Instead of taking great care of current customers, he got
hooked on fantasizing about growth.

When you went to see Pierre about a customer concern,
you saw that he had architects' drawings spread out across
his desk and all over his office. You tried to bring him back
to the present moment, but his head was always in the
future.

Instead of making the most of his current I.T. master
trainers, course creators, and consultants, he began hiring
mediocre surrogates who would learn quickly to parrot the

words of the original trainers so his business could get bigger, faster.

Pierre thought expansion of his business into a bigger building would also be better. But bigger was not better. Bigger became a disaster. The quality of training dropped dramatically. Soon his top trainers were leaving (as they witnessed all the company's money going into all the new expansion), and customers were complaining and not coming back. It wasn't long before Pierre was right back into the failure he had started with. His best people were gone. His best customers were gone. All because he thought bigger was better.

You have huge advantages being small. You can move faster. You can pay more special attention to people. You can get to know your customers on a more thorough basis. The list goes on and on.

So when you expand, be certain you lose none of those advantages! Because bigger is just bigger. It's not always better. In fact, most of the time it's worse!

Remember the law of supply and demand. When you get bigger, you run the risk of violating this law and having more supply than there is demand for. To be truly successful in your small business, you want to reach the point where demand for what you offer is greater than the supply you have of it. That is the road to riches because it allows you to adjust your price upward to meet the demand. (High profit margins first. Expansion second.)

Make *sure* you keep supply and demand in mind at all times. It's a law that will serve you. Forgetting it is like taking a walk on a skyscraper's rooftop and absent-mindedly forgetting the law of gravity.

Supply and demand is why ocean front property is so expensive. There is only a certain amount of ocean front, with an ever-increasing demand. (Have you bought a house in California on the coast lately?) It is why diamonds cost what they do. There is only so much in supply.

If you grow bigger too fast you are no longer a diamond. You are no longer ocean front. You have too much supply, and that will actually turn business away. You don't want all that availability. You want limitation. Limitation increases value.

The bigger you get the faster you lose that advantage.

There is excitement when there's more demand than there is supply. There's excitement in the words "SOLD OUT!" or "STANDING ROOM ONLY!"

What if you took your family to Disneyland and there was no one else there to ride the rides with you? Would the experience be the same? As much as people "hate" those long lines, they still call Disneyland "the happiest place on earth!" and part of that feeling is because it sure feels like the whole world wants to be there at once, and Disneyland can barely handle the demand.

Harley-Davidson motorcycles' profit soared when they ran out of motorcycles and had to put prospective buyers on a waiting list!

There's another reason—equally important—why bigger is not better. That reason is your own personal quality of life. Keep asking yourself, *Why did I want my own business?* And your answer will probably center on control and freedom.

The bigger you get, the less control you have over your business. Soon you are taking on partners and lenders and people looking over your shoulder every day watching their money. Pretty soon your independence is gone, and you spend all your time answering to others! Why? You thought bigger was better.

So stay as small as you want to. Always be full and always be crowded with customers who want your services. That way you can keep your prices high and select the customers you want and not just accept any customer because of a need. When you get blindly bigger, you generate all kind of new needs.

Base your business on wants, not needs, and you'll realize that small is beautiful. You can grow in profitability without growing in size.

74. Sell Something Today

The fact is, everyone is in sales. Whatever area you work in,
you do have clients and you do need to sell.

Jay Abraham

We have people we've consulted with for the last few
years that have terrific ideas, but the problem is, they
haven't actually made a sale.

You can't turn something into wealth if you can't sell it.

When Sam and Val started up their small dance studio
business, they didn't have a commercial space at first. They
started the whole process by renting a room in the community center. They paid $25 to set up a little table there. They
didn't even have the venue where they were going to teach
their lessons!

But after handing out a bunch of flyers they had seven
people show up. They told those people that to get started
at the music studio, there would be $20 registration fee.
And they said, "We'll have to get that *today* to get you started." And they got seven people to give them $20. So they
now had $140!

Sam remembers, "For us to start our business we knew
we had to *sell something today*. We couldn't just leave it out
there like an idea in the future."

Many people we know have new ventures they want to start, but they keep pushing into the future because they're worried about charging people money for it. And so they keep wondering, "Who else should I bring into this business?" and "Do I need to go to some school and get certified before I...?" And they keep creating obstacles for themselves that will put off that fateful day when they might have to sell.

But they need to sell something today! That's what launches it. They need to just do it now and start charging for some aspect of it now to break through that mental barrier.

Steve was working with a young consultant we'll call Drew the other day who said, "What else do I need to do before I start coaching?" He was a very highly qualified person for coaching people, and Steve said, "You need to coach somebody today and have them send you a retainer fee."

And Drew said, "Oh, I just don't feel comfortable doing that. I'm not ready yet. Do you think I should get certified somewhere? Aren't there a lot of coaching schools that would certify me?"

"You are certifiable, yes. But Sam and I have coached hundreds of businesses, over 20 Fortune 500 companies, and no one has ever asked us for our certification. The results you get are your certification. You just have to *do* it! Get on the phone and start coaching. Get the ball rolling. Once they get how good you are, you can then *sell them something*!"

Drew needed them to send him that first check. Because until he did, the dreaming and wishing could go on forever. Psychologically he'd put a barrier up that didn't need to be there.

Back in the days when Sam did door-to-door selling, the sales team would always talk about "breaking the ice." They would need to break the ice by making the first sale. Once they had done that, it became a lot easier to succeed.

There are people who talk about real estate investing, and they've studied information and gone to 50 different seminars, and they've listened to audio programs. But they've never actually bought or sold any real estate. But they consider themselves to be a real estate investor, just by vicariously eavesdropping on the subject.

But are you a football coach because you watch football on TV and say what an idiot the referee is?

Sell something today.

75. Keep Your Eye On the Door

Sometimes we stare so long at a door that is closing that we see too late the one that is open.

Alexander Graham Bell

Opportunity is always knocking. Just answer the door.

There are entire industry categories that didn't exist five years ago. With the internet, the rate of new opportunities opening is amazing.

As an exercise, read the newspaper, follow your internet news site, and watch TV this week with a different mindset. Not just to see what's going on but to play the game of "Where's the Opportunity in This?"

Daniel Pink, who writes about the ever-expanding opportunities for wealth that the future holds, says, "In the industrial economy the tools you needed to create wealth were large, expensive and difficult for one person to operate. But now the tools—such as a laptop—are small, affordable, and easy for one person to operate. I have a modest home office. I've got two computers in this office—more computing power than was on Apollo 11. And the tools and means of production are easy for one person to operate."

Sam was reading the newspaper this last weekend and got to the Arts & Life section, and there was an article about old records. It was talking about a certain record that had a big new cult following. People were searching like crazy for it. So Sam jumped on the internet right after reading that and went to a domain name registration service. He did a quick search wondering if the title of the record was still available as a domain name. And he was amazed that it wasn't taken yet.

This hot new craze was written up in the paper with a circulation of over a million, and because it was an AP story, it must have been in other papers all over. It was a craze someone could turn into a revenue source right away. Even if all you created was a membership forum site that carried ads and paid links.

So how do you identify an opportunity? Look back on Sam's anecdote. The key factor was that people were searching. The key words in wealth opportunity are: searching, seeking, yearning, and longing. People who want something! That will always give you an opportunity to serve. How can you help people get what they want so badly? How could you help people who really want that record and can't find it?

A lot of products and new businesses are started by people irritated because they can't find something, or they can't get a service performed, and so they just decide they're going to start doing this themselves! They can't get it anywhere else. And pretty soon people start buying it from them, and it goes all around.

When you see opportunity, you want to make sure that you see it as an opportunity to serve, as opposed to some get-rich scam. How can you really serve people?

Vinod Gupta began his career working for the then Commodore Corporation, a mobile home manufacturer in Omaha, Nebraska, where he once created a list of sales leads by requesting a copy of every Yellow Pages book in the United States and compiling the information. He gave the list to his boss but stopped in his tracks when he realized the opportunity that was knocking. (*There are a lot of people who could be served by this list,* he thought.) Soon he had received permission to sell this list to other companies, and after a short while he formed an entire company of his own that sold lists called *info*USA.

Today, the company, headquartered in Omaha, Nebraska, has an annual revenue of $311.3 million! It compiles the industry's largest and most accurate consumer and business databases, and it is accessed by more than four million customers nationwide. Vinod Gupta currently serves as chairman and CEO.

That's another example of somebody saying, "I bet people would want this information and could use it!" Vinod was just someone with a regular job who was at his job one day and saw something. Others saw a big pile of discarded yellow pages books. He saw opportunity.

76. Don't Say It's Too Good to Be True

Anything you can imagine is real.

Pablo Picasso

People look at opportunities for wealth creation and think, "There's got to be a catch," or, "You know what they say: 'If it's too good to be true, it probably is.'"

No it's not! Life itself is pure opportunity. And that's true. If you believe that opportunities are too good to be true, you're going to close your mind to your own future.

There was a recent study in *Women's World* magazine (Sam's an avid reader) that said that people who pictured themselves as contest winners actually won more contests. They did a study! But how can that possibly be true?

Well, first of all, the people who picture themselves as winners tend to *enter* more contests. That makes the odds go up right there. Whereas people who say "I never win anything..." never enter much either. Why bother?

Picturing yourself as a winner is how one might explain phenomena like Johnny Cash and Ed McMahon. People like that, with not much talent to begin with, kept auditioning and entering anything and everything until they simply landed on top.

And people shake their heads, "How does he get to be a popular singer?" Or. "How did he get to host that show? How did Ed McMahon get to be so rich and famous? What talent does he have?" Well, he *entered* more often. Audition after audition. And anybody can do that.

Eighty percent of success is just showing up. There's a lot of opportunity that looks "too good to be true." But most of the time it is good, it is true, and it can happen. You just have to stop thinking and saying that fatalistic phrase. It will take you out of the game. You can't win the game of life if you don't play.

77. Pay Taxes Gratefully

Money is the symbol of duty.
It is the sacrament
of having done for mankind
that which mankind wanted.

Samuel Butler

A lot of people automatically think of tax as a bad thing. But taxes result only when you're making income. The truth is, paying tax is a good thing because it means you're making money.

We have both had years when we paid virtually no taxes at all because we were so down and out we had no taxable income! We would have loved to have paid some tax. They didn't even ask!

Tax is evidence of revenue generation, and the more we hate it and try to avoid it, the worse the whole subject pollutes our creative minds. If you can shift your thinking to the positive and pay taxes gratefully, it opens the mind for more wealth creation.

Sam pays a lot of school taxes through properties he now owns, and rather than resent it, he always allows himself a moment to think of all the kids who have schools to go to because of those taxes. When he drives around and sees children in the playground, he allows himself to feel the positive connection to it.

The most important thing about tax is the language you use to think about it. The government can't make you rich and the government can't make you poor. The government is not in control of your financial well-being. You are. The system isn't perfect, but we have an opportunity to create great wealth through the service of others inside this system.

"I used to be a famous complainer about taxes," Sam recalls. "I recently found an old file I had full of information about how I could evade taxes and move to places where there are no taxes! It actually contributed to my fear of success. I thought if I got rich I'd just get soaked with taxes. It wouldn't even be worth it to succeed, because the more you work, the more you're taxed."

Sam started turning his prosperity around when he learned to think the opposite of that. Now he looks forward to paying taxes!

And no matter what you think politically, whether you are in favor of more taxation, or whether you wish that taxes were lower, it doesn't matter. You've got to keep all of that in a separate compartment from how you think about your professional life. Because if you let that cross over and you start to get resentful about taxes, you're going to poison your own thinking, and it's going to bring you down.

Taxes are a sign of success. The more taxes you pay, the more successful you are.

Don't unconsciously fall into the psychological pitfall of having taxation be something that distracts you from what you're really up to, and that is creating even more wealth through ever-increasing, amazing service.

78. Fly and Buy First Class

You cannot spend money in luxury without doing
good to the poor.
Nay, you do more good to them by spending it in luxury, than
by giving it to them;
for by spending it in luxury, you make them exert industry,
whereas by giving it, you keep them idle.

Samuel Johnson

Make sure you are willing to experience how the other half lives or else you may never get there yourself.

Every once in awhile it's good to buy the most expensive version of something, just to learn, first of all, what it feels like to get the most expensive something. Also to experience what it's actually like spending the money and just releasing your anxiety, instead of always thinking, "I can't afford this!"

You will also benefit from directly experiencing how the most expensive thing is made and how it's marketed and serviced. Because if you can get familiar with it, then it makes it less mysterious to you. You can create it yourself that much faster.

Spiritual teacher and author Byron Katie says, "We think that because Gandhi wore a loincloth, and Jesus wore robes, that's how it's supposed to look. But can you have a normal life and be free? Can you do it from where you are? Can you do it from here now? When you're lying on your feather bed, can you be free there?"

Yes.

Sam remembers when he was doing door-to-door book sales, all the other sales people got used to going into the lower-middle class areas. They were just too afraid to go where the expensive homes were.

"And the thing I learned was that if you went into the expensive areas, it's actually not that difficult. The people there were less threatened. They were more impressed by you—just by the fact that you walked up that super long driveway and knocked on the imposing, nine-foot, double-oak doors, they thought, 'Well, this kid probably has something to say that I should listen to.' And they admired the boldness that it took. Sales were easier there. And I think that came from just not being afraid, even at a young age, of the expensive life."

Every once in a while just buy yourself a first class ticket to fly somewhere, just to understand the difference, or stay once in the nicest hotel in town, just to get the experience of it. Not that you have to do it for the rest of your life. And not to be reckless with your money when you don't have a lot. But the experience itself is worth it.

Especially if you're going to learn to market your own service to wealthier people. (You can call it a sociological experiment that you're conducting in order to expand your professional thinking.)

Otherwise, you'll just adapt the knee-jerk miserliness that we've all known growing up with the Depression mentality, and you'll never really know how the "other half" lives. And to create wealth, you'll want to be willing to join the other half.

When Sam was 19, he was doing very well selling books door-to-door, and had some money. His father was turning 50 that year, so Sam went to a jewelry store because he wanted to get his dad something memorable.

"I actually went there to get him a Rolex watch," Sam recalls. "Now, everyone thought I was crazy, but I treasure that experience of just not being afraid to go and blow a whole lot of money on something that didn't make a lot of sense. Because at the end of the day, how many times does your dad turn 50? I wasn't a terrific money manager in college; I just would have blown it on who knows what, anyway. But I still remember doing it, and even though I didn't buy it for myself, I had the experience and the memory of doing it. I think back on that and I think how I did it then, and it kind of showed me the territory that I could be in; and so now that I'm in that territory, it's not like this big, unfamiliar place I haven't been to before."

Like parachuting in World War II: We'll drop you in across enemy lines so you can get to know the lay of the land, and then we'll come lift you out after you've been there a week and you've smeared your face with black, and you've got night vision and you've crawled among the cottages and the forests inside enemy territory. Now we're going to lift you out because now you've got all the maps. That's the same thing! Go do things where the wealthy are because you'll learn a lot.

Go to the most expensive restaurant. If you're afraid of that, that means that's where you've got to start. (Remember: not every night. People go to a B restaurant many times—always thinking they can't afford the A restaurant. But the point here is to skip going to a B restaurant a couple times, and use that money on an A restaurant.)

The great internet wealth guru Matt Furey sends us daily emails that cultivate wealth mentality. You can sign up for them, too, at no charge at www.mattfurey.com. Recently Matt was in the airport on China's Hainan Island, checking in for a flight with his friend and client, Dr. Dave Woynarowski. Dave noticed a Buddhist monk standing in line.

Matt said to his friend, "Doc, I think you may have missed this, so I want to make sure you take note of what class the monk is flying in."

The doctor took a look and said, "Wow, he's flying first class."

"That's right," I said. "And rightly so."

"I also notice he's not carrying his own bags," said Doc.

"Correct. And once again, rightly so. Now tell me, based on what you've heard about eastern religion and philosophy, what is wrong with this picture?"

"Well, it's that in the western world we think monks don't have any money, that they're poor."

"The exact opposite is the truth," Matt said. "In China, and in other Asian countries, the monks are rich. Yet everyone in America thinks they're not. In America we've bought into all this 'money is evil' and 'desire is bad' hokum. People in the U.S. buy into silly ideas that spirituality and money don't mix. Yet the opposite is the truth. When you're always worried, fearful, and anxious about money—how can you truly be spiritual? Your mind is continually clogged with thoughts of lack, of things not being in flow. When you don't have any worries or concerns about money, when your finances are in good order, then every inhale and exhale takes on a whole new life, a whole new meaning. None of your energy is focused on lack; all of it is focused on abundance. So when a monk meditates, it's a totally different experience than when a normal person does. Therefore, the whole idea of giving up money to increase spirituality is poppycock. You integrate the two. You thank God for your blessings, then you relax and take the abundance given to you and use it to improve your life."

79. Read and Grow Rich

Properly we should read for power.
Man reading should be man intensely alive.
The book should be a ball of light in one's hand.

Ezra Pound

Reading is one of the best ways to really get yourself into the flow of wealth creation. (And audio books and audio downloads are abundantly available to those who prefer that to reading.)

There's wonderful material out there written on the subject of what it takes to make money and what it takes to keep money. But a lot of people still don't do any reading. They talk and talk to other failures they know, but they don't do any real reading.

Reading (and listening) are inspiring. Learning how other people have done it can really inspire you and give you fresh ideas about what you could do. Especially people in totally unrelated professions!

A lot of times, you'll be riding down the road listening to a CD of how somebody in a different kind of work got some success going, and you have a business that's totally unrelated, but the idea applies to your own career. All you have to do is make a few changes. So now you bring something to your career that no one else is doing.

We've given you a list of books at the back of this book that have changed our lives and altered our own wealth curves dramatically.

A friend we'll call Jed once said, "I'm just not a great reader. My parents were divorced when I was young. That caused me to become addicted to the television as a companion for myself, and therefore my reading skills are not great. I am just not a great reader, and it's painful for me to have to read."

So we sent Jed a ton of audio recordings that he listened to in his truck and his career absolutely took off. He later started listening from the CD player beside his bed at night and in his earphones on his walks in the woods.

A lot of people think "read" or "listen," and that's where it stops. But to read and grow means when you read something, you actually act on it. And if you read the right things you will! They are so powerfully written that they inspire action. You're not just reading so you can sound smart when you talk. After all, even Shakespeare said, "Action is eloquence."

80. See Into the Future

You are the product of your own brainstorm.

Rosemary Konner Steinbaum

Staying awake to technology is a primary road to wealth. People who saw the power of the internet benefited greatly.

Conversely, many of our clients who refused to adapt to new information systems were later dragged into the future at huge costs to their organizations.

It is not cute or curmudgeonly to hate high tech and do everything the old way. It's lazy. Wealth does not flow freely to grumpy old men.

Ray Kurzweil is an inventor, entrepreneur, and author of four best-selling books, including *The Singularity Is Near: When Humans Transcend Biology*. He has received the National Medal of Technology and is an inductee in the Inventors Hall of Fame. He says:

> "A key point to keep in mind as we contemplate the future is that the pace of change is accelerating. And that means our power to expand the boundaries of human knowledge and accomplishment is accelerating, too. That the pace of change is accelerating may seem obvious, but most people fail to take it into consideration.

According to my models, we are doubling the 'paradigm-shift rate' (roughly the rate of technical progress) every decade, so we'll see twice the change in the next decade that we saw in the last, four times the change in the next 20 years that we saw in the last 20, and so on. The power of information technology is doubling even faster: in less than one year. This means that information technology, as measured by price performance and capacity, will multiply by 1,000 in less than a decade and 1 billion in 25 years."

Be a part of that future. Don't be frightened of it. Join it. Let it fascinate you and embrace you. Use your deep curiosity to spend part of every day exploring worlds that are new to you. Your fear of change won't be seen as a charming "old school" characteristic. It will be seen as fear. Fear turns wealth away. Every time. And love draws wealth in. Every time. So love what's new. Spend enough time with the new paradigm of information technology, and you will expand your mind's receptivity to wealth.

81. Say More Thank-Yous

*It's a little known law of nature that the more
gratitude you have,
the more you have to be grateful for.*

Elaine St. James

We find more secret potential for wealth in untapped gratitude than in any other unturned stone. People simply forget to thank people.

The wonderfully colorful wedding and event planner Colin Cowie emphasizes to Oprah when he visits her show that "It's never too late to say thank you."

We all nod in agreement when the subject is wedding gifts and other social occasions, but what about business? What about professional life?

It applies even more.

The most profound unbreakable law of business we know is this one: *you get what you reward*. But it's also the least used law, even though it has vast potential for increasing your wealth.

If someone refers business to you, how do you thank them? With an email? Of course not. Do you believe if they get 57 emails that day they will treasure yours? They'll be anxious to delete it!

Most people only thank someone once for a referral. Sometimes nicely, with a hand-written note and a phone call. But even in that the potential is missed.

If Thomas refers Elizabeth's company to you as a client, and you do great work for Elizabeth's company, make sure you keep Thomas in the loop! Give Thomas reports on how well Elizabeth is doing! Keep in touch about the referral! Make it a big, big deal. And ask Elizabeth to pass the thanks on to Thomas whenever Elizabeth expresses gratitude to you.

Gratitude is powerful. It leads to repeat referrals. It leads to more of what you are grateful for.

Just recently our client Madison, an attorney with her own one-woman practice in Seattle, had received three referrals of new business from a golf partner of hers. After she spoke to each prospective client, it turned out that there really wasn't a match for Madison to do work for them, and nothing came of the referrals. A week went by and she entered a coaching session.

Madison said, "Those referrals came to nothing."

"That's fine. What have you done to express your gratitude for the referrals to your golf partner?"

"I thanked her at the time, and I thanked her before I called the leads."

"And since then?"

"There's nothing to say! I didn't get any business. It didn't work out."

"Do you want more referrals?"

"Of course. My business, everything depends on referrals."

"So why just do nothing? In fact, doing nothing will increase the odds that your golf partner will never refer again."

"How is that?"

We went on to explain to Madison how people—all of us—make up stories to fill an information vacuum. Because her golf partner never heard from Madison about how the referrals eventually worked out, she'll have to assume (make up a story) that things didn't go well. Or, worse, if the golf partner sees the person she referred to Madison a month later and asks how it worked out and that person says, "It didn't," the golf partner will assume the worst about Madison. She will now be less likely to refer again, which will affect Madison's wealth curve.

Solution?

Gratitude.

To get more referrals from her golf partner, Madison must take one more step (minimum) to ensure that. She must talk to the golf partner (or write to her) thanking her again and explaining *why* things didn't work out. She must emphasize that she only takes a case when she can genuinely help and make a difference, and she never takes a case just for the fee. In these instances after exploring things with the prospective clients, it was mutually agreed there wasn't an immediate need for Madison's services. Madison can then take the opportunity to thank her golf partner again for the referrals and let her know that anyone she refers will be treated with complete care and special attention.

Now the golf partner is happy and relieved that the referrals she made all led to good conversations and were gracefully attended to. The extra gratitude expressed will also prompt the golf partner to remember someone else she wants to refer to Madison so another referral will soon come Madison's way.

When you receive a gift from someone, Colin Cowie says the proper protocol is to send a written thank you note within 48 hours. "That's ten points," he says. "A phone call is nine out of ten. An e-mail, eight out of ten. A fax, seven out of ten. The most important thing is just to acknowledge it. It's never too late—you can do it in two weeks' time, as long as you remember."

In fact, Colin says the first thing he does every morning is write last night's thank you card on his personal stationery.

You'll also find Colin's business stationery at his favorite chocolatier, liquor store, and florist. That way, when he sends someone a box of chocolate, a bottle of wine, or a bouquet of roses, he can dictate a note on his stationery instead of a generic gift card. "I think those details are important," he says. Oprah said when she got flowers from Colin, not only was the note on his stationery, but it was in his handwriting! That's because "I FedExed the note to the florist before they sent the flowers," he explained.

Thank your customers. Thank your vendors. Thank the people who work with you. Thank your family. The more you thank people, the more you yourself will prosper. We've never seen it not work.

82. Find Your Hidden Advantage

Success is achieved by developing our strengths,
not by eliminating our weaknesses.

Marilyn vos Savant

Hidden advantages are everywhere, but hidden. When we get lost in the daily rush, we often forget to step back and study our process for hidden advantages. Step back and look. At least once a day.

McDonald's became one of the largest commercial property owners in the world because they spotted a hidden advantage in the 60s. They realized that just competing by selling burgers and fries against a whole raft of competitors was going to get tougher, and one thing they could use as an advantage was that they could own all their real estate instead of having to always rent. So in the 60s they started buying up all the lots that McDonald's restaurants were built on. And McDonald's today makes more money from real estate, by renting it out to the franchisees that own the restaurants, than they do from the actual royalties on the food sales!

The same thing happened with Wal-Mart. Back in the 60s when Wal-Mart had less than 10 stores and K-Mart had 200 stores, Wal-Mart was a joke. They were the new kid on the block, and they had no advantage because everyone thought the visible advantage was the size of the business. But the *hidden* advantage was what Wal-Mart worked on. They decided that they could skip a major cost of doing business—and therefore increase profits—by starting their own distribution center. And instead of building a lot more stores, like Kmart was doing, they started building more warehouses. Soon they were buying trucks to pick up items from the manufacturer instead of having a trucking company or the manufacturer's own trucking company take it to a middle man who would actually break it into different amounts and then ship it out to different stores. And they had a few more advantages built in, like building a warehouse that you could drive a truck right through so you wouldn't have to take all that time to back it in before packing it up and driving it out. You'd drive right straight-on through, and they would fill your truck up as you were driving through.

Then they slipped another advantage in. Unlike other distributors that were operating on just an eight-hour day, Wal-Mart said, "Why don't we go 24 hours so we can restock a lot faster? We've already got our own trucking systems and warehouses. Why not see the hidden advantage in that? We can make our own hours."

At the end of the day, Wal-Mart cut the cost of distribution from five percent down to two and a half percent and they were able to get their shelves re-stocked in two to four hours when a product was out of stock, as opposed to other stores like Kmart taking four to five days. Now two and a half percent doesn't sound like a whole lot, but when you're talking about billions of dollars, it adds up. Of course we all know what happened to Wal-Mart and what happened to Kmart. By the time Kmart realized that Wal-Mart had these huge hidden advantages, it was too late.

People in small businesses say to us, "What's the great advantage I can have if I really have no advantage?" We say, "You can always outlearn your competitors. You can always have that advantage."

And the smaller you are, the more likely it is that you can develop hidden advantages. Because in very large businesses like Wal-Mart and McDonald's, most of the advantages are advantages of scale, and small businesses can really develop dramatic advantages because there are so many things that they have time to do. Especially with customers. The fewer customers you have, the more you can do for them! Soon you're turning them into customers who refer others and are real excited about who you are. That way you don't have to use so much time and money for advertising. So even being a small start-up can contain a hidden advantage.

Our friend Matt Furey was a world-famous martial artist and collegiate athlete when he began offering his physical training tips over the internet. He also had a hidden advantage: he was a natural writer. Matt had a gift for writing down-to-earth stories and rants and raves about fitness and wealth and motivation. He tapped into that advantage by pouring out an endless stream of fresh and lively daily emails to his ever-growing membership list of subscribers. Other athletes and physical trainers simply didn't have that.

So look into your own life and find the hidden advantages you have, and keep bringing them up to the front of the line to perform for you. We know you have them, because every client we work with has them. Remember that they are "hidden" advantages, which means they might even be hidden from you. So let your coach or partner or friend or sponsor or mentor tell you what they are. You'll be surprised at how many there are.

83. Find Gold in the Yellow

The successful warrior is the average man, with laser-like focus.

Bruce Lee

Countless people with a restless urge to start a wealth-creating venture of their own are paralyzed with indecision. What should I do? Where should I start?

If you just take an ordinary average Yellow Pages book and start looking through it, with laser-like focus, you'll see an astonishing array of business categories out there. And you will also see opportunities hidden inside businesses and services that present themselves in a deceptively boring and mundane way. Don't miss the fact that they have potential for a lot of profit.

Look in the Yellow Pages and phone a few of the places that interest you and notice what shows up at the other end of the line. Many of the places you call do a terrible job of just doing the basics, like answering the phone!

Or, like describing their services in the yellow pages.

If we wanted to start a brand new business tomorrow, even if we didn't know a whole lot about the business, the first thing we would do would be to look in the Yellow Pages and see which categories were popular categories. Then we'd make some calls and find out right away which ones were really being underserved on the customer service side.

One of America's best known hypnotherapists is a friend of ours named Lindsay Brady. When he was young and lost in career indecision, Lindsay found his career by going through an entire yellow pages book and circling the professions and services that struck a chord with him. When he got to the H's he saw "Hypnotherapy," and being curious, he circled it. After looking into it he learned self-hypnosis to cure himself of various fears and weak habits. He was so successful at that he went to school and took up the profession and never looked back. We've written about him in previous books (and list his website at the back of this book.)

If your own brainstorm needs some electricity, pick up your local yellow pages. There's gold in there.

84. Turn Frustration Into Profit

In the beginning I looked around and, not seeing the
automobile of my dreams, decided to build it.

Ferdinand Porsche

It was one of those early summer days in Oregon when
our friend Connie was sitting in her back yard getting
ready to eat a salad. She had recently discovered she was
allergic to sugar, so her mood was not great as she looked
at options for making the salad taste good.

She couldn't use most commercial salad dressings
because most of those have a lot of sugar. So Connie was
trying a store-bought plum vinegar today. She put it on her
salad, and after chewing for a minute she knew it was
awful. The vinegar was harsh and repulsive, and heavy
with salt and artificial flavors.

Completely frustrated, Connie put her fork down and
pushed her salad bowl away. She heaved a sigh and looked
around her yard. Soon she was staring at all of the fruiting
trees and vines in the yard and an exciting question
popped into her mind—what if I could use this fruit to
make my own natural vinegar?

Even though she had no background in these things, and never even spent much time in the kitchen, Connie started experimenting that summer with four kinds of sugar-free fruit vinegars: loganberry, raspberry, strawberry and grape-mint.

"I just didn't like what was out there, and so I started experimenting in my kitchen," Connie said. "The first year I made what I thought was a lifetime supply—30 bottles—and I gave a few away as Christmas gifts. My family was singularly unimpressed, but my friends, on the other hand, immediately wanted more."

In fact they asked her so many times her "lifetime supply" was dwindling to nothing! She told them, "Why don't you go buy your own vinegar?" And they said, "That's the point! We can't. There isn't anything out there that's anything like this." When they said they'd be happy to pay for more, Connie was shocked.

That summer she decided to do an experiment. She bottled 700 bottles (eight different kinds) as a test product while simultaneously completing FDA requirements. To Connie's amazement the "test product" was sold out in no time! She was getting calls from all over the United States and Canada from people who had heard about the vinegars from friends in Portland.

Connie Rawlings-Dritsas is now the owner of Blossom Vinegars, a company that converted frustration into the vibrant experience of summer made with Oregon's finest, freshest whole fruits, herbs, and one Washington onion. Her produce is picked in the morning on Northwest, family-owned farms and is in production by evening.

Customers love the radiant colors, unparalleled taste, and beautiful packaging, all made in Portland, Oregon, with no added sugar, color, or salt. And although Connie can no longer infuse all of Blossom Vinegars with fruit from her yard (this year's production is estimated at 6,000 bottles!), she makes sure to keep it fresh and local. And yes, we use these vinegars now ourselves and even send gift packs to friends and relatives. (Find her at www.blos-somvinegars.com).

Connie is a perfect example of converting frustration into wealth.

Pay close attention whenever you are frustrated by anything. The things that are frustrating you about your business, and the things that are frustrating you about your life as a consumer, could be the very things that cause a wellspring of success.

Frustration is where attention needs to be paid, rather than wishing that part of life would go away.

Recently we went to coach a business owner and we asked, "What's your biggest frustration?"

"It's hiring people. It's so hard to hire good people, and it takes too long to train them. People quit and it leaves us shorthanded, and our sales suffer."

"Great. You've just identified the one thing we're going to nurture here and make the strongest point of your business. Because you're not going to help it out by just making it a little bit better. If you've got some frustration, you need to really convert it into the thing you love the most, and really take it on. The reason it frustrates you is that you're lowering your consciousness every time you confront it."

By raising his consciousness about hiring and recruiting, he made it the very best part of his business and his business took off.

Find what frustrates you, and treat it as a great gift. Because it's the universe telling you something. Frustration is pointing the way. If you take the frustration and make it your masterpiece and turn this into the best part of your life, then everything else will get great.

We always begin our coaching by looking for the frustration. Look for the most stressful thoughts and beliefs a person has. Because we know that's where the access is to a big breakthrough.

Whenever people don't take care of you, when you're the customer, take note of your frustration! Let's say you walk into a store and someone doesn't even make eye contact with you, or they treat the phone like it's more important than you are. All these things that annoy and frustrate you! Make sure when you return to your business that you tell everybody what just happened, and you let them know that this is something *we will never do*; this is just another sign from the universe to show you and annoy you and remind you that you will never do this to your customer. It strengthens you! You just had it done to you, and it was the worst feeling in the world, and you'll never do this.

Don't numb yourself to frustration. Really feel it. Let it wake you up.

Your frustration is actually there to make you rich. If you're having a frustration with something that can be solved by a product, service, or gap in the marketplace, chances are that hundreds or thousands of people in the marketplace or millions of people in the world are having that same frustration! Use it!

85. Open an Easy-Earned Money Account

The rich get richer. Not only because they have surpluses with
which to invest, but because of the overriding emotional release
they experience from having wealth.

Stuart Wilde

Sam was having dinner with his in-laws and when it
came time to pay for the meal, he reached for the check and
said that the meal was on him.

"Oh Sam," his father-in-law said, "we don't want you
spending your hard-earned money on us."

"I'm not," said Sam. "I have two bank accounts. One is
the hard-earned money account, and the other is the easy-
earned money account. And whenever I take you to dinner
I just spend from the easy-earned account. So there's no
need to feel guilty. The truth is it didn't take me any sweat
or any effort to get this money."

They thought Sam was kidding. He wasn't. He actually has an easy-earned account. All the money in that
account is money that he's created from residual income,
no real work on his part, and no active labor. It's often from
commissions he gets from a one-time sale that keep coming

in over and over again, and the account grows every month.

"And it's just a good feeling psychologically," Sam says, "that not all money is hard-earned. You don't have to sweat for every single penny you get. And I think that's been drummed into people from the days of farming when nothing really happened without you directly touching it. If you had a harvest, someone else didn't go and plant extra seeds for you. You dug up the ground, you planted the seed, and you took the crop out and harvested it, and hopefully no inclement weather happened in between. But those were the days when if you wanted milk, you'd have to milk the cow. You'd have to touch and produce every single thing. These days, it's not like that. You can have your own money working for you."

We got an email today from a publisher saying we just sold the rights to Malaysia for one of our books and we'd be making a nice royalty from this. And we hadn't done anything the day we got the email; we just woke up and looked at our computer screen.

Put enough creative joy into a project like a book and it will keep giving back. Long after. And the real joy is that people in Malaysia are now using that book to make their small businesses grow and prosper. We didn't have to go to Malaysia and milk a cow for our part of the money.

It's really good for people to open their mind to that concept and get out of the farming mindset. The agriculture metaphor for making money was probably pounded into them by their parents and grandparents who also gave them the fear of the Depression, and pounded that into them, too. It's time to realize that if you benefit people enough in enough ways, additional wealth will come to you. And it can flow in on your day off.

A lot of people don't take that day off because of the agrarian mindset that says nothing you do has any value or return if you're not actively laboring on it. Yet, because we live in a high-speed information age where imagination is the prime wealth-producing factor, days off and afternoons by the beach *can be* wealth-producing and rejuvenating.

One brilliant idea that serves lots of people can pour wealth into your easy-earned money account for the rest of your life. So let that account live in your mind if nowhere else.

Many people we work with fall victim to the impoverished thought that if they're not actually working they're falling behind. They can't see that a week off from work could be a major jump ahead in wealth because of what it does to rejuvenate the creative part of their being.

86. Move Your Decimal Point

As long as you're going to think anyway, think big.

Donald Trump

As odd as it may sound in a book about wealth, the truth is that we often place *too much* importance on money. By attaching too much emotional charge to it, we push it away from ourselves. We create such severe energy around it, we repel it.

It's better to simply see money as a number on a piece of paper with a decimal point. (As opposed to something you need desperately, or the final validating reward for being a worthwhile person.)

Learn to start thinking and talking about it in simple numerical terms rather than talking about whether you're worth living, or any of the hidden psychological messages people carry attached to money.

You can just talk numbers!

One of the best pieces of advice Sam ever got happened in a job interview. It was one of the few job interviews he'd ever been to in his life. He sat across the desk from a very wealthy man who owned a big company. The wealthy man was the father of one of Sam's friends. One of the hesitations Sam had with taking a sales job with this company was that the selling he would do would be to other big companies and the individual sales would be $100,000 to $1,000,000 sales!

"And my previous sales experience had been selling encyclopedias," said Sam. "Which have a price tag of a few hundred dollars at most. So I told this potential employer of mine that I didn't know how comfortable I was working in this environment! Because I was used to selling items that cost so much less. I didn't know if I could sell something that costs $200,000. I didn't think I could really do that. And he looked at me and said something I will never forget. He said, 'You know, Sam, the only difference is that the decimal point is moved. That's it. In your mind, just move the decimal point. And if you can think of it that way, it won't make any difference whatsoever.'"

Sam said he realized right then that all he had to do was relax and think differently. It really doesn't matter how much money you ask someone for. The key was not in the amount of money but simply the peaceful ability to ask for it.

"The amount of money that you take into your life is really based on how willing you are to ask for that amount," Sam says today. "And how willing you are to simply move that decimal point."

We get subconsciously conditioned early in life to freeze that decimal point. Because as children we were always thinking in terms of pennies. We learned that if we took care of the pennies, the dollars would take care of themselves. We were told that "a penny saved is a penny earned!" So our early parameters were very small. And subconsciously, we never lost them. Our thinking created a paradigm that became a prison.

But a penny saved is still just a penny! So we might want to release that old thinking. A dollar earned is a dollar earned, and a penny saved is a penny saved. Which would you rather have in your bank account? The dollar earned or the penny saved?

And $100 or $1000 earned is a lot more than those pennies would grow to be. But we pretend not to see that. We become shy and retiring about money. People mention a large amount and we blush and bat our eyes as our hearts go racing.

Some theorize that we may have been emotionally sabotaged by the scarcity mindset of the Great Depression. A lot of our money proverbs and sayings came from that era of financial fear and terror. They were well-meant survival-based sayings, but damaging to the psychological relaxation necessary for the creation of wealth. Sayings such as, "Waste not, want not." or "Money doesn't grow on trees" and "We have to be tight and frugal."

These are all good sayings as far as they go. They put the brakes on mental recklessness. But they also put the brakes on creativity. Because for true wealth creation to occur, you want to allow the state of mind that can expand. You want to be open enough to look for ever-larger amounts, and develop a mindset that can easily move a decimal point. You want to *expect* the bigger amounts so that you'll become more comfortable with the bigger amounts of money than the smaller amounts.

Sam remembers when the most money he ever made in one day was $800. A big commission day.

"And I thought that was the most money in the world. And I still remember how I felt, how I jumped up and down, and it was terrific. $800! And now, I'll have days with $8,000, $80,000, $100,000 in one day. If you told that to me 10 years ago, that I could actually make $80,000 in one day, I would have said, 'I don't think I could I handle that!' But now it's a very non-emotional thing; it's like, well, it's just a decimal point anyway."

It's really important to grasp the effect on each and every one of us that the Depression had. Even for today's great grandchildren of those who lived through the

Depression, it still applies. That mood of real fear is still there, that "wealth could go away!" "Watch out, you could lose everything!"

People actually think that the pursuit of wealth itself is somehow going to *cause* poverty! They think, "If I try to make some money, I'm going to lose it all. Look at our neighbors; they tried and they lost their shirt!"

We actually had one of our coaching clients say that. He said, "I'd like to be like you and start a business, but I just don't have a business head; I'd lose my shirt the first day."

And what Sam said to him was, "Why not just buy a lot of shirts?"

Sam has shared in our earlier book, *9 Lies That Are Holding Your Business Back*, that he failed five times in small businesses before he learned to think differently. He was always thinking small in those days.

"I used to look at businesses and think, 'If you can just make a couple of cents off each thing, then it'll really start adding up!' But it turns out that it took too long to add up."

As we consult with our small business clients, we want them to realize that it takes just as long to sell a customer a $30 item as it does to sell a customer a $300 item or a $3000 item or a $30,000 item. The way to cure the irrational fear of thinking big is to just keep moving your internal decimal point. The minute you find yourself at one number, just think, "What if I thought a little bigger than that?"

Never be satisfied with the penny-level thinking. Realize that because of the negative money psychology put into our heads by the Depression, our unconscious tendency will always be to go small. To contract and shrink down. Emotionally, it feels safer and easier. But creating wealth is about replacing the emotional with the logical. So it takes a little push to keep expanding your concept of what your value really is.

87. Ask Above Your Fear

Fear always springs from ignorance.

Ralph Waldo Emerson

What holds a lot of people back from money is just the fear of asking for it. This happens on many levels.

There's fear that if you have a business or offer a service and you raise your prices—and we encounter this constantly with business owners we coach—people will not want to do business with you because you're more expensive now.

The assumption is that the only thing that customers want is low price. It's an erroneous belief! So people, for years and years have kept their fees way too low. They're not able to serve themselves well or serve their customers well. Because they're just afraid of what'll happen.

You face two worlds: There's what you think is going to happen, and there's what actually happens. And what happens in the mind is always worse than what happens out in real life.

Our experience with ourselves and our clients is that raising fees *helps* the business, despite the few defectors that were not your ideal customers anyway.

We had a client named Drake do this recently. Drake raised his prices, and out of more than 300 regular customers, there were only three who left him! And if we'd asked him before how many he thought would bail over the new fee he would have said 50 to 100!

The key is to just condition yourself to have your fee reflect your ever-increasing value to people.

Take a deep breath, and ask for something above and beyond what your fear tells you not to ask for. And keep doing it, because now you've created a new game and a new level for yourself. Like Ralph Waldo Emerson said, "The greater part of courage is having done it before."

Every day you're delivering something better than you did yesterday. You are better today than you were yesterday. If you are not, you shouldn't be in the line you're in. And if you're better every day, then why isn't your fee rising accordingly? When a company gets better, the stock price keeps going up, so your own prices need to go up, too; and if they're not, you have a great opportunity to increase your wealth.

88. Don't Look in the Obvious Place

Just one great idea can completely revolutionize your life.

Earl Nightingale

You might want to look for something that *doesn't* look like an opportunity. That would be your real opportunity, because you're the only one looking there.

You'll remember in the early 80s when VCR's came out and we started renting movies. Soon the market was over-serviced by a factor of ten! There were 10 times as many video stores as there had to be for the actual market out there. Because everyone was jumping into this hot new opportunity.

The same thing happened in the mid 90s when every single person was starting up a coffee shop because cappuccino was the hot new craze.

Any time we've seen something that's supposed to be the "next great thing" and jumped on the band-wagon, we've paid a price. Because that hot thing is so obvious, and everyone's talking about it, we joined an over-crowded field. A day late and a dollar short.

Look at real estate. We have people look at us with a twinkle in their eye and say, "Don't tell anybody; I'm getting into real estate! The housing market. It's huge." And we say, "Okay, we won't tell anybody."

The real road to wealth stretches inside you. From your mind to your heart. It's internal. What can you be passionate about? It's not something external that everyone else is greedily jumping on.

89. Don't Discuss Your Plan

Action is eloquence.

Shakespeare

Put your creative energy into the work, itself, instead of talking about the work.

Talking takes a lot of energy. Boasting takes even more. That energy is precious.

If you're telling everybody what you're going to do, then you're not listening to them. And opportunities for improved success reveal themselves, not when you're talking, but when you're listening. No one ever talked themselves up to a new level of consciousness.

Opportunities reveal themselves when other people are being vulnerable and talking and telling you what they're looking for, what they're hoping to achieve, and what they're involved in.

Because all of a sudden you'll hear something in their words that is in alignment with what you're doing, and you will make a connection with that person that leads to something very good for your business. That can't happen when you're talking.

It has to happen when you're open, listening, and welcoming.

Sam gets real curious about people and asks them about their lives and learns a lot from them. And they feel impressed by him and close to him, and a lot of people even ask him after the conversation, "Will you coach me? Will you help me?" And that's not because he said, "I'm a big, successful business coach." It's because he asked questions.

Boasting about your own plans puts pressure on you and the plans. It shuts down your ability to listen and keep the plan flexible. The other downside about broadcasting your future to others is that naysayers will feel threatened by the fact that you have a plan and they don't, so they'll shoot it down. Warn you off. Caution you in the name of love.

Keep your biggest ambitions secret and exciting. Let people *watch* them evolve. Stay in action. One minute moving your plan forward is worth a thousand minutes of talk.

90. Ignore the Experts

Let us resolve to be masters, not the victims, of our history, controlling our own destiny without giving way to blind suspicions and emotions.

John F. Kennedy

Sam remembers being frightened by the experts. They were saying that Generation X would be the first generation *not* to do as well as their parents financially.

Sam panicked.

Prior to Sam's generation, every generation had done better than their parents financially. They've been able to ride the elevator up. The economy was always expanding and the country was doing well, and new products and markets and services were being developed and people were succeeding all through the 60s, 70s, and 80s.

But once we hit the 90s, the experts said, "It's done. You kids now are on the downward spiral; we've pretty much peaked."

Sam remembers thinking, "Wow, that's not good. Too bad I was born too late! If only I'd been born a bit earlier I could have had it as good as my parents had it. But the experts say there's no hope, because this generation just won't do as well as their parents."

But it hasn't turned out that way.

Sam's done much better, not only than most people's parents have done, but sooner than their parents had done it. What has taken a lot of people to the age of 50 or 60 to accomplish, Sam did by the time he hit 30. Now Sam teaches others.

"Ever since I met Sam my own business has taken off," Steve says. "His enthusiasm for these ways to create wealth was absolutely contagious, and I started applying them left and right. I don't regret not doing it earlier. I'm just grateful for everything now."

So what about the other experts? Why do we ever listen to them?

Any time the real estate market or the stock market gets a little bit hot, the experts say, "It can't last; there's going to be a correction. It's the bubble." There are experts always predicting that the next Great Depression is right around the corner. The end times are always near. People have been predicting doom since the beginning of time. More than 2,000 years ago the prophets were warning that the world would end in their own literal calendar lifetimes. Oops! Didn't happen. (Where's the apocalypse we were longing for?)

Remember that the experts who are paid the most attention to are the ones who've got the most negative predictions. Because the media will not get ratings from the headline "Things Are Great as Usual!"

But if somebody says, "Watch out! Within a year all the banks are going to be closed," that paper will sell out; that show will top the charts. The whole concept of "selling" news is centered on dire warnings and shocking scare tactics. Ratings come when viewers are upset or frightened. That's what gets people to watch. People use the media as kind of a warning system. Just for a thrill.

Therefore, the media seeks experts who come with dire predictions; that's who they seek out! And they give us a false impression that these are all the "real experts." These experts are saying that this prosperity can't last, and our dependence on this resource is going to cripple us as a nation, and things don't look good. The planet is in trouble.

But we don't understand what the media is really selling here. They're selling fear. We think they're selling reality.

Katie Couric is in the same business that Freddy Krueger is. And if we don't really understand that and grasp it, we're going to have a hard time creating wealth, because we're going to be scared all the time because we're believing the experts.

People think everything is limited and there are so many constraints that they better be careful. Experts in the media tell them all about limitation all day. Soon they're trapped in the finite fallacy. Don't let this happen to you.

Tune into the infinite. Realize that the universe is evolving in ever-increasing abundance. That is its nature. Listen to your inner wisdom. That's the only expert you'll ever need.

91. Turn on the Speed

Time has more value than money…
you can get more money but you can't get more time.

Jim Rohn

Whatever you've got going on, continue to speed it up.

Many fundraising organizations that we have coached, for example, improve their fundraising results by speeding up the thank you and receipt process. A simple, small thing, but donors feel so much more appreciated when they get their acknowledgments immediately instead of days or even weeks later.

Many people get busy during the day and actually work against wealth by trying to figure out how long they can get away with not responding to a communication. What can we get away with? What does the customer expect, and how long can we actually wait before we get something back to them? And they try, actually try, to stretch it out as long as possible, not realizing that any time you can do something faster, the customer benefits and starts recommending you to others.

So when you get really good at responding quickly and take the position that says, "We're not the cheapest—but we're the fastest," you can keep your service at high alert and charge people more because people love speed. Time is the new money for so many people!

People can send letters by regular mail, but often choose to send things by Fed Ex because speed has such a value these days. If you were going to get into certain types of businesses, you would always have the advantage if you could be the guaranteed speed leader. Think of the frustration attached to something that is slow or takes forever—what would people be willing to spend for a guaranteed speedy completion? FedEx itself created its wealth by asking this very question.

How can you be faster at what you do and make a game of it? Don't make it a burden, but have fun with it because it can astonish people and bring wealth your way.

92. Specialize in Specialization

You do not merely want to be considered the best of the best. You want to be considered the only ones that do what you do.

Jerry Garcia

When you can specialize in something you'll speed up your road to success.

A lot of people are coaches today. And recently we went to a website of someone who is a "retirement coach" who specializes in coaching retirees on how they can have a wonderful life after work.

We just thought, "How brilliant is that?" because retirees do have the money for life coaching. And they certainly have the time! And people who were defined by their roles as professionals or parents can lose all identity in retirement. They don't know who or how to be! Perfect opening for a specialized coach.

Teaching people how to have an enjoyable retirement is a terrific specialization. If someone had just been a "life coach" going into a retirement community saying, "I am a life coach," they would probably say, "Why do we need a life coach? Our lives are almost over! And what is a life coach anyway?"

Anytime you can specialize it draws people to you. People are willing to pay a higher amount of money for specialization. Don't limit your income by trying to be all things to all people. Don't come from the need-based mentality that tells you you can't afford to pass up anything. Don't have your business card read, "I'll just do anything for anybody!"

We coach people starting a business who are focused on that "needy" part of the worried mind that prompts them to put up a sign that says "No job too small!" Knock that off.

When surgeons specialize the price goes up. A visit with a medical specialist will cost a lot more than a general practitioner. A brain surgeon gets paid more than a GP. So the more specialized you are, the higher the value of your time and your service.

Can I be the only person in this industry who does something? We know a lawyer who specializes in elderly people who are going through Alzheimer's issues. You can get lawyers anywhere, but how many lawyers specialize in people going through Alzheimer's? And if this guy costs more than a regular lawyer, you feel he's worth it.

When Jerry Garcia of the Grateful Dead said, "Be the only ones who do what you do," he knew what he was talking about. If you have a Porsche and need to get your Porsche repaired, and you're driving along and you see "Porsche repair" and on the next block you see "car repair," you'll pull into "Porsche repair" because you feel those people are really going to know your car. They do Porsches all day and they may cost a little extra money, but they're not going to make the mistakes that the other people make because they don't know your car. So in the long run it will cost you less money.

Contrast that with the sign that says (and we've seen them!) "Car repair, specializing in foreign, domestic and other cars!" That's not specialization at all.

So don't be afraid to have a specialty. It's also a wonderful way to focus on what you love to do—to become a specialist in it!

93. Give Yourself a Year

People never plan to be failures;
they simply fail to plan to be successful.

William Arthur Ward

If you're in debt or have a severe lack of money—and we've both been in that situation—to think that you're going to solve all your problems in a month is unreasonable. That thinking will ultimately backfire.

Instead, learn to think in terms of a year. Not overnight success, but a very good year. Allow yourself a full year to make substantial progress. And if you're in debt, just the simple act of writing down all the things you owe at the beginning of the year (as small and minute as they are) will help you get started. Because as the year starts you'll be going down that list and crossing things off as you take care of them. That's the excitement of doing that kicks in right away.

We both have lists of goals going back many years, with the yearly goals now being more than 10 times what they once were. It's amazing the change that will happen from one year to the next if you're focused on allowing your *one good year* to happen.

When you're looking towards a one-good-year wealth creation, be open to the question, "What can I do to create it?"

And this one-year miracle can be performed in jobs, too. You don't have to be an entrepreneur. Many of our coaching clients have day jobs, and they create one-year money miracles there, too.

Our friend Stephanie recently was working for a framing company that had a certain amount of standard pay for the position she was in. But she kept increasing her skills and the amount of value she was providing to the owner with her work, even though there was no real reward in sight. And when one day her immediate supervisor left the company, they immediately put Stephanie in that position. So now she's doing both jobs: the job she used to do, and the management of the department. She already proved to them she could do it. And as Napoleon Hill said frequently, "The man who does more than he is paid for will soon be paid for more than he does."

Keep increasing your value to whomever you work for. You don't have to know exactly where your future wealth is going to come from. You can have a job with a large company and create wealth for yourself.

Yet some people say, "But you don't understand. I'm in a business or company where my boss just doesn't appreciate me and he's a big idiot." Even so. If you create more value that you deliver to your company, even if it's not appreciated at the company you're in, it will always pay off. If your attitude is one of a continuous value-creator, you will always get offers from people who notice that. And your skills will build exponentially.

We recently went into Office Depot and saw a happy, energetic lady working there and we thought, "Wow, this person is doing something that she might think is mundane, but her attitude and the get-it-done happy energy is amazing. This is the kind of person we want!" She joined our team a few months later.

Our former client and friend Karl was a service tech at a copier company who set out to become a sales person within a year and make nice commissions. He did exactly that. He was patient enough to have it occur over a year's time of work and study and contribution. Two years after that he was a sales manager! Give yourself a one-year money miracle project and patiently execute it.

94. Just Take the Next One

When one door of happiness closes, another opens;
but often we look so long at the closed door
that we do not see the one that has opened for us.

Helen Keller

Don't worry about lost opportunities. They don't mean a thing. People give them way too much meaning and drama, and it brings them down and renders their thinking impotent.

We were driving in a lovely part of town with our depressed friend Gregory who said, "Wow. If I would have bought three houses in this area 20 years ago, *then* I would have been rich.... I guess I missed the boat."

Gregory didn't realize that there are boats waiting every day. If you miss one, you can take another. You don't have to take all the boats. Just one will get you where you want to go. Boats are opportunities, and they are always appearing to the person who is ready to sail.

But people like Gregory would rather talk about the "once in a lifetime" opportunity. They don't realize that there is no such thing. If you miss your own "once in a lifetime" opportunity, celebrate. The next one is going to be even better.

Bing Crosby had a once in a lifetime opportunity to have a huge hit record when someone played him a demo recording of "Rudolph The Red-Nosed Reindeer." Bing thought the song was childish and would never sell. He rejected it. Later it was recorded by Gene Autry and the rest is history. But Bing Crosby only laughed about it later. There were other opportunities, always waiting.

In fact, in the right frame of mind, anything at all can be an opportunity. In this frame of mind you'll never worry about "lost opportunities" because you'll start to realize that opportunity can never be lost. Why? It is a creation. It's not an external event.

For example. Fred DeLuca was a teenager who borrowed $1000 to start a sandwich shop with his friend Peter Buck in Bridgeport, Connecticut. They called their little shop, "Pete's Super Submarines." Prior to opening the sandwich shop, Fred DeLuca had never even made a submarine sandwich for himself or anyone else.

Fortunately for him, Fred did not fall victim to the myth that says, "It takes money to make money." (This myth is actually one of the nine business lies we write about in *9 Lies That Are Holding Your Business Back* and *The Small Business Millionaire*.) Nor did he worry about being too young or too old or anything else. He wanted to make money to help himself go to college, and so there wasn't a lot of room in his head for worry.

Although Fred DeLuca started very small, his sandwich chain is now all over the world, described by some as the most successful franchise business of all time. Is there anyone who has not enjoyed a delicious Subway sandwich made to order? Subway uses the advertising slogan "Eat Fresh" to explain how every sandwich is made on freshly baked bread, using fresh ingredients, in front of the customer to their exact specification, by employees who Subway terms "sandwich artists."

Notice that Fred DeLuca did not have to catch a once-in-a-lifetime opportunity to succeed. In his own words, anyone can "start small and finish big." Anyone.

Today it's even easier than back in 1965 when Fred opened his sandwich shop. Today you have the internet. The global marketplace is at your fingertips.

In the past when you had an idea of some kind, or wanted to market a product or service, there were all kinds of hierarchies and people you had to impress. You might have had to get the word out into the media. (If the newspaper decided not to cover you, you were out of luck.) You had to go through a lot of layers to have people know about your business. But with the internet now, the world is flat; and if you've got a great idea, within 24 hours, you can have half the world already knowing about it. Internet word-of-mouth travels in a heartbeat.

So people right now are even better poised to make that next opportunity work. You just need one. And you can create it out of anything. Like Fred did out of a sandwich. Focusing on all your past missed opportunities will keep you from being open to the next one right in front of you.

Finally you begin to realize that there's no such thing as a once-in-a-lifetime opportunity. Even though that's the talk you hear wherever people gather: "Yeah, you know, did I ever tell you I had a chance to buy into that company? But I didn't do it. Yeah, I was offered this opportunity one time and I passed it up. Oh, man—that was my one shot. Because I blew it on that one, I guess that was it. It can never happen again."

There's a great example locally here. There's a guy we've met who started a company called 1-800-got-junk. He's Brian Scudamore. He dropped out of school when he was 17 to start a company that would pick up big items that you would have to take to the dump. If you had an old couch that you couldn't throw in the trash, Brian would come get it. Or if you had useless items in your basement and you were cleaning it out, and you didn't own a truck, you'd have to get rid of them somehow. So you would call Brian.

Brian had a used pickup truck and just started this service of taking things to the dump for people. And his parents thought he was crazy for dropping out of school. And that didn't really seem like something that would really impress a lot of friends. Like, "Hey, I'm a junk man!" Yeah, like Sanford & Son.

But he kept serving.

Brian's company today is pushing $100 million. Now it's turned into something he calls the "Fed Ex of junk removal." And he's been profiled on *Dr. Phil*, and he appeared on *Oprah*—a guy picking up junk, appearing on *Oprah*! Brian appeared on *Oprah* and took his company to $100 million because his mind knew of no such thing as a "lost opportunity." The concept doesn't exist for him.

95. Get Rich Quickly While Getting Rich Slowly

Slow motion gets you there faster.

Hoagy Carmichael

A lot of people want to get rich quickly. Which is fine, actually. Breakthroughs often happen quickly. But while you're making bold moves, you can also get rich slowly in a parallel universe.

Have a system in place that makes an automatic monthly investment that builds wealth for you. It can be one of those automatic mutual funds that you buy as a long-term plan that promises, "In 35 years you'll have a million dollars if you follow this plan." Those programs aren't exciting on the surface, but they give you the mental freedom to take bigger chances in your other universe.

Because you don't always have to sell your cow and squander all the money on the magic beans. We hear people say to us, "I spent my life savings on this project!" without seeing that such a move is self-defeating. If you take your life savings and put it all into one thing and you blow it, it'll stop you from taking chances in the future ever again. And maybe it was that next chance in the future that was the right one for you. Not this one.

The real payoff to having a wealth-accumulation plan in place is not when it matures many years away, but rather right now in the moment. The psychological release you get from fear is powerful, and it frees your mind and spirit to really love your work and take it all the way.

The peace of mind you get from the slow-accumulating account is not from the money. It's from the faith.

96. Create a Physical Equivalent

Inward calm cannot be maintained unless
physical strength is constantly and intelligently replenished.

Buddha

When you've got a big financial goal that you're up to,
you can reach it faster by asking the question, "How do I
create a physical equivalent of this goal?"

Don't leave your body behind in your pursuit of prosperity. The body can help you. Remember the whole system is mind, body, and spirit. And whole systems succeed
faster than partial, broken-off systems. A fractured system
will collapse.

Sometimes people get so obsessed about a mental goal
that they don't even think of creating a physical equivalent
for it.

But wealth flows to something more than just the mind.

Your body can generate enough energy to be an attractor
force of its own. People with healthy bodies, for example,
don't need as much sleep and they can think more clearly.

Even if you're in a wheelchair, you can create a physical equivalent by increasing your breathing exercises and

doing things that make your lungs larger and bring more oxygen to the brain. Even singing will create a dynamic physical equivalent.

Your mind becomes stronger when your body does. It comes along with it, and it's better able to build wealth into your life. There are benefits to being strong and healthy. People see a spring in your step and they want to be with you; people are drawn to people who aren't just shuffling along with no connection to their bodies.

So if you set a goal to double your income next year, make sure you create a physical equivalent to that. Do something that will increase your strength or your endurance or increase your energy or your physical ability to keep up with the financial goal you've hit. Set that goal, too.

Some people use the word "bodymind" to anchor this issue. The Greeks used to say that the key to success was "a sound mind in a sound body" and they were correct. The two go together.

Sam says, "I like the quote, 'Your health is your wealth,' because if you don't have the physical ability to function, you don't have anything. If you're too weak to make a fist, you're not going to go knock 'em dead."

97. Create Team Spirit

The main ingredient in stardom is the rest of the team.

John Wooden

Your teammates don't do good work when they surrender and become unhappy. They don't think of fresh ways to help you. They don't make the customer want to come back. In fact, if you get enough unhappy players on your team the whole mission can fall apart.

So their happiness comes first. Before money. Before success.

Most people have this process completely reversed in life. When you ask them why they would like to succeed financially, they say because it will make everyone happy. But the opposite is true. As the happy people in Seattle's fish market proved, happiness leads to money, not the other way around.

Professional golf is considered to be a serious sport full of concentration and discipline. Yet the great golfer Ben Hogan said his formula for success was to "Be absolutely determined to enjoy what you do."

Most of us are not like Ben Hogan. We wake up and surrender to the hardships of the world. We get out of bed and wave the white flag of defeat. All power is conceded to the outside: outside circumstances, family members, spouse, co-workers, customers, people of all kinds. Whatever they want. Whatever makes them happy.

The problem with that surrender is that we lose our self-esteem over it, and we lose that sense of inner freedom that gives us energy for life. We lose all of it.

A friend sent us this passage from a book by Dr. Seuss because he said it reminded him of what we had been coaching him out of. This surrender thing we do.

"You have brains in your head,
You have feet in your shoes,
You can steer yourself any direction you choose.
You're on your own now and you know what you know
And YOU are the one who'll decide where to go!"

In all the years we have worked with sales people we have found that the greatest predictor for sales success is personal happiness. Most people say that it's commitment, or drive, or purpose, or self-discipline. It's not.

So have the fist step you take each day be the happiness of yourself and everyone you work with. Start with your team. They are your internal customers. When they are on edge it makes you wealth-repellant. Light them up and customers will be drawn to that light. The team (including you!) comes first. The customer comes second.

98. Use Your Imagination

Thought is the original source of all wealth, all success,
material gain, all great discoveries and inventions, and of
all achievement.

Claude M. Bristol

A few months ago Sam and his wife Val were going for a
drive along a waterfront area just outside of Vancouver.
One of their favorite drives has a beautiful view of the
water and the spectacular mountains of British Columbia.
They came across a sign advertising three acres of waterfront property for sale. The price tag was $1.5 million.

Did they have $1.5 million burning a hole in their pock-
et? No. So instead of using money, Sam decided to use his
imagination to see how they could buy the property.

Sam called the seller at 9:30 that night and asked about
the property. They met the next day and over lunch Sam
told him his story.

Sam recalls, "I had to sell the seller on *me*. On wanting
me to have the property. On working with me to buy the
property."

By being creative they reached an arrangement to
give Sam time to space out the purchase of the land so he
could swing it. The unexpected bonus was that the seller

accepted an offer to partner with Sam and invest in another real estate project he was trying to find partners for.

You can always use your imagination to create real wealth, not just fantasies about the good life. When you tell successful people your story and your goals, it's surprising to see how many will want to help you.

The three-acre property will be the site of Sam's new home but will also house a waterfront meeting center Steve and Sam will use for coaching and sessions to help others create wealth in their lives. Sam has named the breathtakingly beautiful property "Creators' Landing."

You can create the wealth and the life you want. If you come to Creators' Landing by the big river in Vancouver for one of our seminars, you'll see living proof that the principles we are talking about in this book work. The power of human imagination.

At a class reunion Sam talked to someone who had become a lawyer. His first thought was "This guy has it made!" But soon the guy was telling Sam about how unpleasant it was to be a lawyer. The guy hated it.

"It's such high stress," the lawyer said, "and there's an incredible amount of work to do. I feel like I'm going to have a heart attack any day. You can't believe the physical duties I have to do every single day, the types of people I have to talk to, and the amount of paperwork I have to fill out!"

But there were ways that lawyer could have circled in on loving his work, if he'd stayed open, optimistic, and upbeat. If his language hadn't become so defeatist about it, he could have found—even within the law—something that was less stressful to him. There are many different kinds of law you can practice. You can be everything from a flamboyant, in-front-of-the-jury showboat who doesn't have to do a great deal of homework, to someone who sits at a computer and does research and filing. And the whole spectrum in between.

But he had shut down his imagination.

When we talk to people who want more wealth, we'll first ask them to use their imaginations.

"What do you like to do?" we ask. And they might even say, "I like hanging out, watching movies, and sitting on the couch." And unfortunately we haven't figured out a way to get paid for doing that. (Although a friend started a blog that contained her movie and TV reviews that has started making her money—so we don't rule anything out!)

Do you enjoy talking to people on the phone? Do you enjoy working on the computer? Do you enjoy doing crafts and building? Writing? Do you enjoy doing things that help other people?

You can start in the most general category in the world. Do you like communicating? Do you like helping? Do you like technical things? Do you like to work with your hands? Don't get overly specific at first. Some people think they have to have a specific vocation call to them, like knowing from birth they want to be a rodeo clown or a ballerina or a fireman. You don't have to pin it down; you just have to start getting closer. Circle in on your prey like a great speckled bird.

99. Honor Yourself

Wealth is the ability to fully experience life.

Henry David Thoreau

Fear of money often causes us to treat each other like frightened, dependent children.

Money can do that in our society.

Case in point: *The Houston Chronicle* reported that bankrupt Northwest Airlines Corporation sent a memo to their workers who may no longer have jobs. In the memo, the company advised workers on ways to financially survive.

One idea they recommended was to "fish in the trash for things you might like!" They also suggested that you take your date for a walk in the woods instead of spending any money.

The memo was called "101 ways to save money." And with that mentality it is not surprising that Northwest went bankrupt.

Northwest spokesman Roman Blahoski said some employees who received the handbook had taken issue with a couple of the items. "We agree that some of these suggestions and tips...were a bit insensitive," Blahoski told Reuters. "If you have saved some money, pat yourself on the back—you deserve it," the memo reads. "Take out only what you need and spend prudently."

But you don't have to treat yourself like an undeserving child when it comes to money. You deserve plenty of money. You don't deserve a life in which all your meals come from the trash and all your dates are in the woods.

Stop wondering if you "deserve" to be wealthy.

You don't question whether you deserve other things. Why just money? If somebody hands you a cold glass of water when you are thirsty, you never think, "I wonder if I deserve this water." When you need something to write with and someone hands you a pencil do you think, "Okay, thanks, but do I deserve this pencil?"

Why then, when somebody offers you a large amount of money to do something, do you immediately feel you might not deserve it?

A lot of us carry low self-images out of childhood. Well-meaning parents have told us, "You're never going to succeed because you don't even know how to clean up your room. You didn't give your schoolwork much of an effort, so you're probably not going to make much of yourself." Consequently, you come out of childhood, quite often, thinking, "I better get some kind of job that makes a minimal amount of money, given how unsuited I am to success."

And that doesn't serve you to feel *unsuited* to making money. It doesn't serve others either. No one wins.

You *know* you have something that you are really, really good at, and when you get it in alignment with a profession that serves others, you will make a lot of money at it. And you'll deserve every penny.

100. Move Into the Light

There will come a time when you believe that
everything is finished.
That will be the beginning.

Louis L'Amour

Steve was just back from Vancouver, Canada, where he
spent two days with Sam who lives there and gives seminars there for small business owners. He had spoken at
Sam's seminar and got to spend time with Sam plotting
their next work together.

Sam's father is from Jamaica, so Sam is, technically, a
black man. He is light skinned, like Harry Belafonte, or
Colin Powell, and he has a Canadian accent. He loves his
heritage and was delighted to point out that he and Steve
could be packaged as a white guy and black guy, like Mel
Gibson and Danny Glover in *Lethal Weapon*. (Now you see
on the second edition of our *Small Business Millionaire* book
cover that we are described as "The Lethal Weapon duo of
Business Coaching!")

Steve says, "I rather liked being Mel Gibson in this
combo until Mel was arrested for drunk driving and it
came out that he was wildly offensive to the arresting offi-
cer and made a number of anti-Semitic remarks about the

Israelis. Two days later he apologized and went into treatment. For alcoholism. So maybe I am Mel after all."

Places like Vancouver always feel so lovely: rain-drenched and dappled in shades of green you never see in Arizona. So Steve's travel there is good. It refreshes. But we also don't want to miss Ralph Waldo Emerson's point about how much we shape our traveled-to beauties by our inner life and perception. Rain can be overdone. It can get dreary. So many songs tell you. Here's that rainy day.

Steve says, "I forget and take for granted the magnificent light in Arizona. Ever see the native Americans do a sand painting? Glorious. They take a fistful of rust-colored sand and let a stream come out on top of an ivory mandala of sand, and soon every shade of light in the world is being eaten and reflected by the sand."

Wealth is everywhere.

Emerson said, "To the dull mind, all of nature is leaden. To the illumined mind the whole world sparkles with light."

The illumined mind has shifted to the light.

Once many years ago when he was depressed about not making enough money in his business, Steve talked to his friend and mentor Steve Hardison. Hardison said to shift your mind you might want to simply shift your body into the light, literally.

"He recommended I get out of Wayne's World (my nickname for the office I had in my garage) and into the outdoors in order to experience more light. More light on the outside, more light on the inside. So I reluctantly followed his advice and started doing my work out on the back patio in the sun, and it shifted! My mood picked up and I started having the conversations that generated new business."

So let's travel to India now to follow this thought through. Not literally, but through the Indian poet Tagore who said, "Faith is the bird that feels the light and sings when the dawn is still dark."

Faith is the bird that we wish we had in our hand. It feels the light. The bird doesn't see the light yet, but it *feels* it coming. You can feel success and happiness coming (Hint: it's already in you; that's why you can feel it!) even though you can't see it yet—you can't see hard evidence or money in the bank. But you can feel the light. You can just feel it coming. So you sing. You sing in the dark. Or you dance when you don't feel like it. Or the doctor tells you your depression will be helped if you just get... just get... just... JUST GET UP! And walk. Which is dancing. It is. (Watch Fred Astaire walk. Watch him just walk!) Faith is the bird that sings in the dark.

You are like all those amazing entrepreneurs who know they have something, but the money is gone. Yet they labor on! They're making their product anyway! Faith is what they have.

Faith is the bird that feels the light.

About the Authors

Sam Beckford

Sam Beckford is the founder of eight small businesses. The first five were massive failures. After business number five he decided to get a "real job" but thankfully got fired after five months and started business number six which made him a millionaire. Sam has shared his business strategies and philosophy with thousands of other small business owners and has personally helped hundreds of business owners across North America increase their personal income by an additional $40,000 per year while working less. Sam lives in Vancouver, Canada, with his wife Valerie, daughter Isabella, and son Ben. He is the co-author of the bestseller *The Small Business Millionaire*. You can get information about attending Sam and Steve's *Creating Wealth* seminars at **www.stevechandler.com**.

Steve Chandler

Steve Chandler is the author of *The Joy of Selling* and over a dozen other international bestsellers in the personal growth field. He has coached and trained over 30 Fortune 500 companies and hundreds of small businesses. He was a visiting lecturer in the Soul-Centered Leadership program at the University of Santa Monica, and lives in Arizona with his wife Kathy and their pet cat, Grizzly Bear. You can reach Steve at **www.stevechandler.com**.

Recommended Reading

The Max Strategy by Dale Dauten

The Master Key to Riches by Napoleon Hill

Work and Money by Byron Katie

Loving What Is by Byron Katie

Creating Contagious Leadership by John Hersey

Customer Astonishment by Darby Checketts

Frankenstein's Castle by Colin Wilson

Creating Affluence by Deepak Chopra

Getting Everything You Can by Jay Abraham

Money: An Owner's Manual by Dennis Deaton

The Trick to Money is Having Some by Stuart Wilde

RelationShift by Michael Bassoff

The World is Flat by Thomas Friedman

You Can Have What You Want by Michael Neill

How to Solve All Your Money Problems by Victor Boc

The Small Business Millionaire by Sam Beckford and
Steve Chandler

Recommended Websites

Steve Chandler: **www.stevechandler.com**

Abraham Maslow, Dale Dauten, Colin Wilson, Steve
Chandler,
eBooks, audio: **www.reinventingyourself.com**

Matt Furey: **www.mattfurey.com**

John Hersey: **www.johnhersey.com**

Tom Peters: **www.tompeters.com**

Darby Checketts: **www.customerchampion.com**

Jay Abraham: **www.abraham.com**

Connie's Blossom Vinegars:
www.blossomvinegars.com

Michael Neill: **www.wealthcatalyst.org**

ROBERT D. REED PUBLISHERS ORDER FORM

Call in your order for fast service and quantity discounts
(541) 347- 9882

OR order on-line at **www.rdrpublishers.com** *using PayPal.*
OR order by mail: Make a copy of this form; enclose payment information:
Robert D. Reed Publishers
1380 Face Rock Drive, Bandon, OR 97411

Note: Shipping is $3.50 1st book + $1 for each additional book.

Send indicated books to:

Name _____

Address _____

City _____State _____Zip _____

Phone _____Fax _____Cell _____

E-Mail _____

Payment by check /__/ or credit card /__/ *(All major credit cards are accepted.)*

Name on card _____

Card Number _____

Exp. Date _____Last 3-Digit number on back of card _____

	Qty.

100 Ways to Create Wealth
by Steve Chandler & Sam Beckford . . . . $24.95 _____

The Small Business Millionaire
by Steve Chandler & Sam Beckford . . . . $11.95 _____

The Joy of Selling
by Steve Chandler . . . . $11.95 _____

Ten Commitments to Your Success
by Steve Chandler . . . . $11.95 _____

RelationShift: Revolutionary Fundraising
by Steve Chandler & Michael Bassoff . . . . $14.95 _____

Customer Astonishment: 10 Secrets to World-Class Customer Care
by Darby Checketts . . . . $14.95 _____

Other book title(s) from www.rdrpublishers.com:

_____ $ _____

_____ $ _____